Creating The Breakthrough Portfolio

Strategies for Managing a Successful Career

Ken Thurlbeck

THOMSON

DELMAR LEARNING   Australia   Canada   Mexico   Singapore   Spain   United Kingdom   United States

Creating The Breakthrough Portfolio

Ken Thurlbeck

Vice President, Technology and Trades ABU:
David Garza

Director of Learning Solutions:
Sandy Clark

Managing Editor:
Larry Main

Senior Acquisitions Editor:
James Gish

Product Manager:
Jaimie Weiss

Marketing Director:
Deborah Yamell

Marketing Manager:
Penelope Crosby

Director of Production
Patty Stephan

Production Manager:
Andrew Crouth

Senior Content Project Manager:
Tom Stover

Content Project Manager:
Nicole Stagg

Technology Project Manager:
Kevin Smith

Editorial Assistant:
Niamh Matthews

Library of Congress Cataloging-in-Publication Data:
Thurlbeck, Ken.
  Creating the breakthrough portfolio / Ken Thurlbeck. — 1st ed.
    p. cm.
  Includes bibliographical references and index.
    ISBN 1-4018-5897-X (alk. paper)
1. Photography—Vocational guidance.
2. Photography—Marketing. 3. Art portfolios. 4. Artists—Vocational guidance. I. Title.
  TR154.T58 2006
  741.6068'8--dc22   2006022621

NOTICE TO THE READER

To Ann, Mercedes, Vienna and Dia.

Contents

Chapter 6   **The Career Path**

Chapter 7   **The Digital Portfolio**

Preface

Intended Audience

Creating The Breakthrough Portfolio is an invaluable reference book for photographers, designers, illustrators, art directors, copywriters--in fact, anyone who needs to present examples of his/her work to sell their work, solicit assignments or gain employment. The book contains tips and suggestions from recognized industry leaders and information and processes that can apply to someone building their first portfolio as well as a working professional who is looking to take their career to the next level. It is meant to be a reference guide that will remain with you for years and help you to continually develop and refine the way that you present yourself in your chosen industry. It is filled with advice and suggestions to help you move your career forward.

Emerging Trends

Computers and digital presentations have raised people's expectations. What was acceptable few years ago now seems outdated. While the idea behind a sample remains important the quality of the presentation is critical. Another key element to a presentation that has gained importance is the consistency of the voice or brand. A portfolio today must define the type of work that you do and want to do while clearly differentiating you from your competition. When you leave a prospect's office you need to have communicated who you are and why you are better suited for the work than your competition.

This trend will continue and as competition increases the professionalism with which you approach the market, from the way you prepare your portfolio to how cleverly you take advantage of search technology to lead people to you, will be critical to your success.

Background of this Text

Over the past several years I have noticed a common question emerging at art director clubs, photography associations and illustrator guilds, etc.: "What can I do to separate myself from the competition?"

An industry of consultants has grown up around advising individuals on developing their portfolios. I am constantly asked to review portfolios and help people build presentations that get them work. I have been fortunate to have worked on several different sides of the business, being a creative director and brand strategist in agencies and design firms as well as working as a commercial filmmaker and photographer. I have spent hours pouring over portfolios both online and offline looking not only at the work but at the way the work was presented. I have closely examined the impact of one presentation method over another and I share the conclusions I have drawn. In researching this book I spoke to dozens of people who make their living reviewing portfolios and recommending people for work. I asked them the same questions I had asked myself and share their insights in this book.

"How do I start?" This is one of the questions I am most often asked when someone is developing a presentation for their work. Over the years I have developed a system that others have found very helpful and that you can use as a guide. This system, included in this book, will lead you along a logical path that will help you define you vision or brand and develop a presentation that will be consistent with it. It will help your presentation speak with a clear voice and differentiate you from others.

Textbook Organization

Creating The Breakthrough Portfolio is arranged in a systematic way to lead you through all the steps you need to consider to create and market an awesome portfolio. Included throughout the book are tips, suggestions and advise from leading industry professionals.

Chapter 1, Getting Started

Here is a quick overview of the market with ideas for you to consider before you actually begin putting your portfolio together. It will introduce you to the concept that a portfolio is not only a portfolio but part of a marketing plan to help you position your work and yourself to achieve your goals.

Chapter 2, Creating Your Vision

What do you want from your career, how do you position yourself to get you there and how do you communicate this to others? Simply put, a few great pieces of work in a portfolio isn't enough to create a breakthrough career--you need to differentiate yourself among your competition.

While this may seem obvious many people have a hard time defining their direction, creating a personal brand and finding a way to communicate it to others. This chapter is devoted to helping you set yourself apart from the competition by creating a personal brand that will set you apart and help you define the direction of your career.

Chapter 3, The Professional Portfolio

Custom portfolio manufacturers give us an inside look into the way they approach building portfolios for their clients. A tour of the portfolio building process from one of the most respected custom manufacturers, **The House of Portfolios** is included.

Chapter 4, Making The Portfolio

It's time to begin assembling the portfolio. There are many things to consider and this chapter addresses them all. The different methods and formats to present the work are examined. What is the experience that one wants to communicate and how does it support one's personal vision? From choosing paper, mounting techniques, pagination, all this will be explored.

Chapter 5, Marketing

A portfolio is only one part of the equation--what you do with it and how you do it after it is built is important if you want to succeed. This chapter helps you construct a marketing plan to open doors and bring you the attention that you deserve. It also helps you lay out a plan to succeed once you have identified an opportunity.

Chapter 6, The Career Path

A career is a journey. It is necessary to know where you want to go and how to navigate along the way. Careers have a habit of taking unexpected turns, some for the better some not. The decisions you make and the people you meet can make the difference between a good career and a stellar one. Here are a few suggestions and tips to help you get started on the right path.

Chapter 7, The Digital Portfolio

The digital portfolio takes many forms: from CDs, DVDs, thumb drives to websites, some choices are better than others. It is becoming more common for the website to be the first introduction of your work, but a website is not enough. How the website works as part of an overall strategy is addressed.

Resources

A selection of places to go and things to think about to help you improve your career.

Features

The following list provides some of the salient features of the text:

* The text is specially designed to apply to a broad range of creative professions, from photography, illustration, and art direction to graphic design, new media, the fine arts, and more

* The information provided applies to creative professionals whether they are first entering the business or trying to reach the next level in their career

* Showcases examples of successful, inspiring, and inventive portfolios with rich visual illustrations

* Engaging assignments and exercises help creative types refine their portfolio to best reflect their personal vision and talent

* Includes a process and information to help the creative individual successfully position themselves in the market

* Includes tips and insights from leading industry thought leaders

DVD

Attached to the inside back cover is an informative DVD full of valuable information including;

1. Interviews with industry experts.

2. A tour of **The House of Portfolios** one of the leading manufacturers of custom portfolios with interviews.

3. *Creating your brand.* A brief look at the process for defining your brand.

4. A look at and discussion of different portfolios

5. Creating pages and assembling the physical portfolios

E. Resource | This guide on CD is developed to assist instructors in planning and implementing their instructional programs. It includes sample syllabi for using this book in either an 11- or 15-week semesters. It also provides chapter review questions and answers, exercises, PowerPoint slides highlighting the main topics, and additional instructor resources.

ISBN: 1401858996

Acknowledgments

I would personally like to thank all those who contributed to and supported this book, as well as all of those who spent endless hours listening to me talk about it: Jim Gish, Jamie Weiss, Stephen Pite, Dave Mandel, Peter Beard, Diane Fields, Colleen Beckett, Ian Sami Hajar, Chie, Ushio, Susan Freldman, Kevin Wassong, Marc Hauser, Kristen Fauling, Brian Ponto, Binnie Held, Drew Stalker, Nina Edwards, Rick Zalenski, Maria Isabel Marcet, Thomas Lombardo, Jason Brown, Susan zCoutler-Block, Martin Kellersmann, Phil Growick, Tnna Rupp, Tom Messner, James Hudson, Rosa Vila Auge, Chip Forelli, Zave Smith, Paul Mathew Woods, Hitomi Watanable, Farah Qureshi, Hal Curtis, Tom McGhee, Alison Stephen, Abel Lenz, Diane Kirkwood, Jib Hunt, Patrick Dorian, Leela Corman, Lisandro Molina, Frank Veronsky, Celeste Celaino, Tanda Francis, Maki Kawakita, Colin Finlay, Lyle Owerko, and Michael Costuros. I'd also like to thank Robert Park, my high school Librarian who instilled in me a love of books that has continued to grow every day of my life, and everyone else who's support made this book possible.

Thomson Delmar Learning and the author would also like to thank the following reviewers for their valuable suggestions and expertise:

David Baird
Southeast Missouri State University
Cape Girardeau, Missouri

Marilyn Ebler
New Mexico Junior College
Hobbs, New Mexico

Therese LeMelle
Katharine Gibbs
New York, New York

Michael Libonati
Art Institute of California
Santa Monica, California

Briar Lee Mitchell
Art Institute of Los Angeles
Santa Monica, California

John Tilton
Katharine Gibbs
Piscataway, New Jersey

Frank Varney
Art Institute of Colorado
Denver, Colorado
Ken Thurlbeck, 2006

Questions and Feedback

Thomson Delmar Learning and the author welcome your questions and feedback. If you have suggestions that you think others would benefit from, please let us know and we will try to include them in the next edition.

To send us your questions and/or feedback, you can contact the publisher at:

Thomson Delmar Learning
Executive Woods
5 Maxwell Drive
Clifton Park, NY 12065
Attn: Media Arts & Design Team
800-998-7498
Or the author at: ken@kenthurlbeck.com

About the Author

Ken Thurlbeck is an award winning creative professional who has worked nationally and internationally. He has held several positions including International Creative Director of Grey Advertising in Europe, SVP Creative Director at Digitas, Creative Director/ Brand Strategist at Avenuea/Razorfish, Chief Creative Strategy Officer at POPstick. He is a noted filmmaker and photographer. He developed Café Films, an international television commercial production company, and directed over 1000 television commercials. Ken has directed several documentaries including, *USSR&R, Rock on a Red Horse*, a documentary about the youth movement in the Soviet Union and how it influenced the country's move towards democracy. This film premiered at the Sydney film festival and garnered many accolades and was widely shown including being broadcast on MTV. His list of awards include many Art Director Club awards, Clios, Lions, Caddy's, Webby's, The Pollack Krasner foundation grant and the Lucie.

His work is collected internationally and appears in many collections including The Museum of Modern Art and Metropolitan Museum in New York, The Stedelijk Museum in Amsterdam, The Walker Center in Minneapolis and The Polaroid Collection.

Ken is a member the Advertising Photographers of America, The Director's Guild of America, The Art Director Club of New York.

His Lectures have included The Art Center in Pasadena, New York University, Perdue University, The University of Minnesota, UCLA, The Director Guild, The American Cinematique, Katherine Gibbs and The New York Film Academy.

His Work appears in the *Digital Designer*, *Nudes form the Polaroid collection*, *Emerging Bodies* and *Photo-dependent Sculpture*.

Ken graudated form York University in Toronto, Canada and also did a Fellowship in Computer Sciences at the University of Southern California.

CHAPTER 1

Getting Started

You might be one in a million, I was

Sometimes you get notified about an assignment or job that you really want. I got one of those by e-mail. I was asked to prepare a submission for a great project with a great advertising agency. I wanted it. Grabbing the phone, I made an appointment and started to prepare for the meeting. Sorting through a pile of my award-winning work, I knew I could win it. The week before the interview I took extra time, carefully arranging my work and mounting it in a beautiful, new, black, distressed-leather portfolio case that I had purchased specifically for the meeting. I also stopped by a signage company and had them cut my logo out of vinyl, which I applied to the outside of the portfolio. On presentation day, I slipped into a new four-button black suit with a black-on-black silk-screened t-shirt and topped off everything with my red-framed eyeglasses. I was one in a million.

Arriving at the agency, on time, I was greeted by a receptionist with a British/Brooklyn accent who told me the interviews were running a little behind. I was directed to wait in one of their glass-walled conference rooms. The room contained a mammoth table made out of some material that had been invented for use in the space shuttle (or on the new Mini Cooper SC, the sign on the wall plaque wasn't all too clear). Enough black Aeron chairs surrounded the table to seat an entire small Baltic republic. I joined a group of five, wearing the requisite creative uniform–black suits and dresses, black shoes, and black portfolios–all waiting for the same interview.

We each got 15 minutes to show our work and pitch ourselves for the job. When my turn came, the creative director flipped through my portfolio asking a few questions and nodded, I thought, in the appropriate places. He was professional, wrapping it up in exactly 15 minutes. "Nice work, thanks for coming. I still have a few more people to see before I make my decision." "By the way," he said just before I exited through the door, "cool glasses."

I had arranged to meet my mother for lunch that day at her favorite Tribeca restaurant. Over the seared tuna salad and cold gazpacho soup, I eloquently reconstructed the details of the interview. "You always have the nicest glasses," was her response. "But you should have seen me! I looked good, did a great presentation, and had a fabulous portfolio. I was one in a million," was my response. That caught the attention of our waiter who, I must confess, had been most attentive through the whole meal. I later found out that when he saw my portfolio, he thought I could secure him a gig as an actor in a television commercial. Waiting on tables was only what he did while waiting for his big break. It is amazing the prestige that you will command when you bring the right portfolio to the right restaurant. "Well," he said, "You may be one in a million but in America that means there are another 260 exactly like you." He was right.

One more thing, your competition is no longer just national. Today, more and more, your competition is international. Companies want great talent–no matter where in the world that talent may be found. Websites make finding talent easier and faster. Talent is also searching internationally. I recently posted an advertisement on a local community e-billboard for an action script specialist and awarded the assignment to a programmer in Japan who answered the ad. Now, calculate those odds.

Did I get the project?

That night when I returned home after the first meeting, I made a thank you card. I designed the card to look like an eye chart. You know, the ones that start out with one large letter on the top of the page and end with a tiny line of type at the bottom of the page. The copy thanked the interviewer for his time and ended with my phone number.

I then laid my pair of red eyeglasses on the chart and photographed them together. I sent a printout of the chart in a large envelope that I designed to look like an eyeglass case.

Two days later I got the call I wanted.

I spent a lot of work and energy preparing for the presentation. Was doing all that work worth it? It was to me, but you'll have to decide for yourself if it is worth it for you. I am not an exception. Many times I have looked for talent. I hire people who show me that they are interested in going the extra mile to work with me.

The reason behind the breakthrough portfolio

I have reviewed a mountain of portfolios and helped many creative individuals build breakthrough presentations whether in the form of a portfolio or Web site. As a vice president creative director with several leading advertising agencies, I have waded through portfolios, CD-ROMs, DVDs, and Web sites to find the right individuals for positions. I have also developed presentations for my own companies. This book represents my thoughts and experiences along with the insights of other industry leaders.

> **NOTE:** Throughout this text I will use the terms *book* and *portfolio*. These terms are interchangeable in the industry. As in, "Do you have a great book?" What is important is not whether you use the term *book* or *portfolio*, but that whatever samples you use in your book or portfolio are all great.

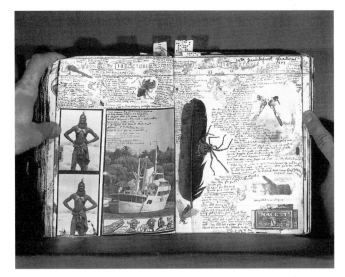

FIGURE 1.1

Photographer Peter Beard has made a successful career of doing the unexpected. I remember seeing one of the images, a self-portrait with him lying in a crocodile's mouth. These three pages from his diary/portfolio are examples of how he approaches the presentation of his work. Along with his own photographs he includes examples of other images and ideas that influence him. One of the first photographers to treat the presentation of portfolio work in this manner, he offers the viewer insights into how he works and what is important to him in his work. Looking at his presentation one can conclude that Peter brings ideas, vision, personality, and a strong sense of design. Your portfolio is not only about the work you have done; it is about how you think and what you are capable of doing.

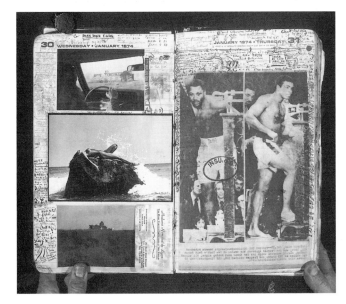

This is a book for people starting out in the business and for people in the business who want to take their portfolio to the next level. The process for creating a breakthrough portfolio and personal brand is the same and is discussed in the following pages.

The Internet has added another dimension to presentations. It can help open doors, but it can also close a door even before you have the chance to talk with someone. More people are requesting to see work online before deciding to meet with you in person. Another expectation is that if you pass the first stage of inspection, your presentation during your interview should reflect the work that was seen online and opened the door.

> ## TIPS FROM THE PROS
>
> "I can't tell you the number of people I interview who walk into my office, sit down in front of me, and never say a word. I feel like asking them, "Why are you here?" I expect that when candidates comes into my office they will look me in the eye, introduce themselves, and hand me their resume. Then I know they are serious about getting a job."
>
> *Diane Fields,*
> *Independent Creative Manager*

What is a breakthrough presentation? Very simply it is a portfolio that stands up and announces, " Stop. Look no further because I am the one." You could use it to get a job, a grant, an assignment, an exhibition, and a proposal or at any number of occasions where you might have to show your work. Some people find their way to a great portfolio easily and others struggle for years and never seem to achieve what they need to build one. A breakthrough portfolio is one that separates you from the others. The examples in this book reflect many different levels and represent work in different stages of careers. The one thing that they do have in common is that they represent people who are presenting a consistent vision. These are people who stand out from their peers.

I am continually asked if I have seen any great books lately. Most creative people don't get the opportunity to see a lot of different portfolios. The reason for this may be that the competition does not want to give away any secrets but sometimes it is just a lack of confidence in their own work. Whatever the reason most people rarely see the portfolios of their competitors. One of the best ways to see someone's portfolio is by showing yours first.

Although there is no one right way to build the right book, there are a number of steps you can take to ensure that you create a portfolio that will make you competitive in the market place. This book will address the steps that you should consider to create a great presentation.

This is your opportunity to see what others are doing

You may have noticed that this book is heavily illustrated with examples of strong portfolios. Undoubtedly you will find some more to your liking than others. One of the most important things to see is what others (i.e., your competition) are

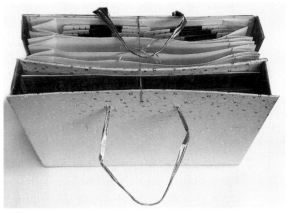

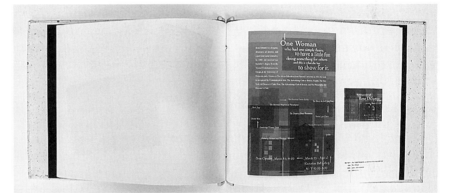

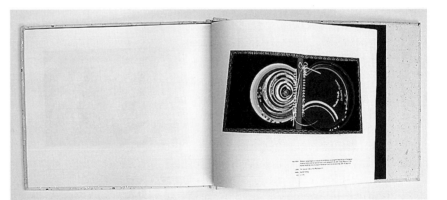

FIGURE 1.2

Colleen Beckett has found a very tactile solution for her portfolio. When you open her portfolio, it is like opening a present and finding a wonderful surprise. Although it requires a little more to get into her work, she has made the journey interesting.

doing. I hope these examples will give you lots of inspiration and ideas for your own portfolio.

I have also included a variety of portfolios from different professions because I believe that inspiration can come from anywhere and the more inspiration and ideas that you have, the better your portfolio will be. But wherever your inspiration comes from, it is important to make your portfolio your own. It should show a clear vision. It should reflect who you are. I will discuss how to develop your vision and lay out a plan to help you find it in Chapter 2.

When Tom Messner went out and bought a portfolio for one of his first interviews, he did not have enough work to fill the book. There was one extra page. Chewing a wad of gum, he sat staring at the page pondering his next step, as the deadline for the interview loomed closer. Suddenly, inspiration hit. He plopped the gum in the middle of the page, wrote a great headline, and stuck it on the page. He had created an advertisement for a chewing gum and a story the interviewer would not easily forget. Tom got the job and now runs his own agency. Maybe you have heard about it: MVBMS/Euro RSCG. A portfolio is a statement about you—a statement that will leave an impression. You must be sure it leaves the impression that you want it to leave.

You are creative, right?

Of course you are creative and that is exactly why you have chosen to do what you do. Whether you are a photographer, art director, writer, graphic designer, illustrator, multimedia designer, architect, environmental designer, production designer, or any other member of the professional creative community who needs to show samples of your work, to get a job or assignment you will need the right portfolio.

Yet, (let's see a show of hands), how many of you have all this amazing, great, creative, exciting work sitting in the typical black portfolio? Sure, there are plenty of reasons to put your work in such a portfolio. Here are the top three reasons that I continually hear:

> They are easy to find. You can buy them at any neighborhood art store.
>
> They are easy to find. You can buy them at any neighborhood art store.
>
> And, they are easy to find. You can buy them at any neighborhood art store.

Right?

What does a portfolio say when it arrives on someone's desk? "Look at me, over here in the pile. I'm just like everyone else." This does not mean that you should

FIGURE 1.3

The black bag, A standard in the industry and just the thing that you want if you want to look like everyone else.

never use black, but if you do, what else can you do to make it break away from the others out there? Even if you are on a very tight budget there are ways to help set your portfolio apart. So do not accept the first solution that comes across your path.

I have been in offices where there have been over a hundred portfolios leaning against the wall, stacked on chairs, and piled on desks. These represent literally a sea of black, simulated-leather cardboard portfolios all piled up waiting their turn to be reviewed. Eventually, someone will go through them all. But look over in the corner, there is a portfolio wrapped with a section from an outdoor billboard poster. Which one do you think would catch someone's attention and be the first portfolio to be opened?

If your portfolio stands out, so do you

Recently I visited a direct-mail advertising agency. Staff from these agencies are the people that create the stuff you find in find your mailbox everyday, from the letters telling you when Ed McMahon will be in your neighborhood with your million-dollar prize to coupons for discounts on anything you can think of. There is so much bad work landing in mailboxes every day, it takes a real creative talent to produce work that cuts through all that clutter.

The creative manager had 30 positions to fill and was reviewing somewhere in the neighborhood of 500 portfolios. She called me over to look at a portfolio. The individual had designed his portfolio to look like a postal carrier's pouch. Her response to this person's presentation was, "this person wants to work here." And he is working there now.

Your portfolio is your ambassador. It can and will open doors.

The creative manager then showed me a portfolio that must have seemed like a great idea at the time. It was a spring-mounted portfolio that shoots the work out across the table each time it is opened. It was left to the viewer to reassemble the contraption for the next victim. Fun the first time, maybe, but imagine someone presenting this book to several time-strapped creative directors over several meetings. Some types of fun wear out faster than others.

Thanks. Nice work

You will rarely have someone sit down with you and discuss your presentation after they have seen it. You will know a good presentation because it will get you the job.

In a presentation that bombed you will only get a polite decline. "Sorry nice work but this is not exactly what we were looking for."

So before you walk out the door with your new presentation tucked under your arm, ask yourself a few questions:

1. What type of work do they do?

2. Who is my audience?

3. What position are they considering me for?

4. What is the impression I want to leave?

Your book is what will get you to the next round or not. If you are lucky enough to accompany it to the interview, you can use your charm and personality to make an impression. But even if your first interview is in person, your book may still end up circulating to others without you present. Usually, the viewing of your portfolio will precede your personal interview. Your book will have to speak for and about you.

FIGURE 1.4

Chie Ushio has carefully orchestrated her book to create a creative page-turner. The interesting graphic on her cover immediately grabs attention and encourages viewers to turn to the next page.

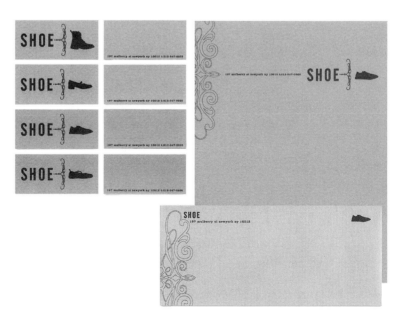

Now some good news

There are a lot of bad portfolios out there, in fact not just bad, but downright awful. In fact, some are really horrible. A friend of mine, a very good art director earning a six-figure salary, came to me because he felt he wasn't getting the attention he deserved. His portfolio contained laminated pieces of his work on black matting board, all displayed in a custom-made box that was stored in a custom-made canvas bag. To his credit, neither the box nor the bag was black.

The work was great, but when the viewer opened the box he or she was presented with about 35 pieces of varying shapes and sizes floating loosely around in the bottom of the box. This was not how the portfolio was originally designed. Originally it had contained 15 numbered samples all mounted on the same size matt board. However, over the years pieces had been replaced with new work. The quality of the new work was great and the art director assumed everyone knew his reputation, so the portfolio was becoming an afterthought.

For a presentation, he of course, arranged the work in the order he wanted it viewed. The problem was, although he carefully orchestrated the order of the work for maximum impact, it inevitably did not remain in the original order after the first viewing because he could not be there every time it was viewed to ensure that the order stayed the same. The last person who looked at the work would usually replace the work in an order that was different from that originally intended by the owner.

The box and the carrying bag looked as if it had been around the block not once but a couple of times, and in several neighborhoods. When I asked him about this, his reply was that it had cost him a few hundred dollars to have everything made up several years ago. Now, this was a guy who wanted to make a major a move and achieve a salary increase, yet he was concerned about spending a few hundred dollars on the one thing that would open this door for him. The problem when you received his package was the statement that it made: "Here was some nice work from someone who didn't care that much about his work."

He kept getting passed over because people felt that they had seen the best he had to offer. When he finally got serious about his portfolio again, editing his work, and having a new portfolio built, his phone started ringing again.

If your work doesn't seem like it is all that important to you, would someone give you one of his or her important accounts to work on? The answer is that they would not.

Your portfolio is an investment in your career. It shouldn't be thought of as an afterthought.

If your work isn't important to you, it won't seem important to the person to whom you are presenting it.

When you are looking for a job or assignment, your portfolio should be the first thing that you think about, not the last. Remember that your portfolio is your own personal ambassador—your own sales representative. It can open the door or make sure you never get through the door.

FIGURE 1.5

Portfolios come in all shapes and sizes and all types of material. Here is one in Plexiglas and another in wood from Lost-Luggage.

I have seen portfolios covered in fur, rubber, rusty metal, and almost any material that you can imagine. I have also seen Web sites that have complicated splash pages and animation and obtuse navigation that is more frustrating than it is interesting. It is important to have a portfolio that breaks through the clutter. If your portfolio *is* the clutter, it won't work for you. If you have a presentation that does not support your work or vision, it will not open the doors to get you where you want you to go.

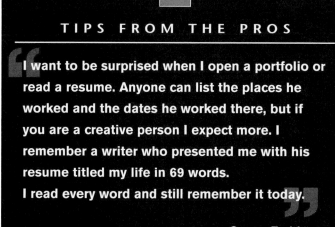

TIPS FROM THE PROS

"I want to be surprised when I open a portfolio or read a resume. Anyone can list the places he worked and the dates he worked there, but if you are a creative person I expect more. I remember a writer who presented me with his resume titled my life in 69 words.
I read every word and still remember it today."

Susan Freidman,
Professional Recruiter

Now the bad news

As the competition increases, it is important to remember that there are a lot of really outstanding portfolios out there. More people are realizing the importance of a strong presentation, and the bar raises higher and higher daily. Some schools have developed awesome programs around creating very good marketable portfolios. Fortunately, the tools to make an awesome presentation are affordable and available to everyone—especially if you live near a Kinko's or have a friend with a scanner and color printer.

And everyday the programs are improving to build a killer Web site. The responsibility to be awesome falls squarely on your shoulders. Fortunately there is help.

There are no excuses

If you wrote a killer headline, but the client uses the one he wrote instead, you don't need to put his version in your book. You go to the digital files, swap headlines pull a print and you have a stronger presentation piece. Need a great photo or illustration? There are stock companies that are just a click away on the internet and they offer a plethora or images on all subjects. A photographer or illustrator may let you use one of their images or you can make a trade and do a promotional piece for them in exchange.

The business you are in or about to enter is a business of collaboration, so collaborate. Collaborate with whomever to build the best presentation that you are capable of building. Need a flash expert, ask around eventually you will find one who is willing to help you. While you are adding to your list of collaborators in your Palm Pilot, remember that you are also building your network. This is a network that will stay with you throughout your career.

You are expected to build the best presentation you are capable of building. No one will hire you because you tell him or her you can do great work without demonstrating that you have done great work. The control is in your hands and, as I will remind you as you go through this book, if you have to apologize about a piece of work it shouldn't be in your portfolio.

Getting the work you **want**

A breakthrough portfolio is a tool. It helps direct you to the type of work that you want, the kind of work that excites you, and the type of work you do best. In fact, without a clear answer to the question of who you are and where you want to fit into the market, the market may define where it wants to put you instead.

A portfolio lets people see how you think. Too many careers remain unfulfilled or die because they are left to happenstance. Do you want to do the type of work you want to do and the type of work you are most successful doing or just the work you happen to fall into? You may feel a great accomplishment just landing any job or any assignment, but if you do not have a long-term plan, sooner or later you will find yourself locked into a small career box that is very hard to escape. If you are not in a situation where you can produce your best work soon, you will find your work will stand out for what it isn't rather than what it is. Your work will suffer as will your career. People around you will consider your work inferior, which it may be. You will find yourself looking for your next job samples that will not get you a position where you can produce your best work, and the cycle will repeat itself.

What you will discover as you read this book is that creating a breakthrough portfolio is not only about putting a selection of outstanding work in a portfolio

TIPS FROM THE PROS

There are a lot of portfolios out there with good work but it isn't enough. I look to see if the portfolio communicates a personality, something that tells me something about the person who created it. I have to get a feeling of who this person is and how he thinks. If the portfolio can do this it will make me interested in meeting this person.

Kevin Wassong,
President, Minyawville Publishing and Multimedia

or on a Web site, it is a process. This process does not stop with the completion of a single portfolio but continues throughout your career.

Work hard, have fun

The creative field is one of the most competitive professional arenas there is and definitely one of the most exciting. By applying the principles in *The Breakthrough Portfolio,* you have already taken a very important step to give yourself a competitive advantage. *The Breakthrough Portfolio* is an in-depth approach to creating a great portfolio *and* a successful strategy to support the portfolio and your professional career goals. It will take time, creativity, patience, attention, and thought. It cannot be done overnight. But if you have a 9:00 AM appointment tomorrow to show your portfolio, pop over to the "do's and don'ts" pages (at the end of this chapter), and good luck. But after the interview, come home, roll up your sleeves, and spend the time that you need to build your breakthrough portfolio. It won't be the last time you do it, and you'll be ready for the next time you need it. After all, this is an investment in yourself and your career. You may find that you may need more than one portfolio as you meet with people who have different needs and as you look for different projects or jobs. An art director for an ad agency will have a different presentation than a designer for a design firm, even though many of the samples could be the same.

And, remember your portfolio is alive. Yes, alive. It will grow as you grow professionally, becoming deeper, richer and better.

Know to whom you are talking

You will present your portfolio to creative directors, recruiters, creative managers, creative group heads, submissions officers, creative judges, account executives, chief executive officers, chief financial officers, business owners, and many more people. Each will look at you and your portfolio differently, and everyone will have an opinion. Everyone will have to make a decision: Is this what I need? You will need to understand who your audience is, what they are looking for, and what voice is needed to reach them. An owner of a company hears what you are saying differently than a creative director does.

The creative director will appreciate that the art director spent an extra 5 hours kerning and leading the typography to help the rhythm of the visual. He would say, "Here is someone who really cares about the details and is willing to go that extra mile to make it perfect." The owner of a company might take the extra time spent to mean that you are looking to add a few more dollars to his

FIGURE 1.6

This is a beautiful aluminum carrying case. It does a great job at protecting any portfolio that it houses. This is a very durable solution, but you would want to be very careful if you were sliding it across some beautiful wooden desk or conference table. Studded, rusty riveted metal portfolios can be remebered for the wrong reason. A creative director had interviewed with several people in an agency and as a courtesy was asked to meet with the agency's CEO. The CEO asked to see his portfolio and the creative director took it out of his bag and slid it across the table to the CEO. A series of deep scratches followed the metal riveted portfolio across the table. The creative director saw he had made a mistake and immediately suggested he would have the table refinished. The CEO was visibly upset but didn't say anything, looked at the book and excused himself. I heard this story from the CEO. He said that yes he was upset because of the damage to their new conference table but more upset because the creative director did not think about the results of his actions before doing what he did. That was not the type of person he wanted responsible for the accounts of his agency and in fact this person did not get the position.

bill. A better way to present spending extra time on refining the work to that owner might be a statement that it is a powerful ad for his or her product and you are making the final adjustment to make his or her publication deadline.

It is your responsibility to communicate to your client in their language. A recruiter listens for different things than does a creative manager than does an account executive than . . . well, you get the picture. You are in the business of communications. It is your responsibility to understand the language they are speaking. Take a few minutes before every presentation and ask yourself what is the key function of the interviewer's job and how can you show him or her through your portfolio how what you do would help them.

The information that is presented in this book comes from years of experience; not only mine, but the experience of other successful professions in the field. In an effort to make this a valuable tool for you, I interviewed people from every side of the creative sphere, from agency chairmen, to creative managers, to creative directors, to recruiters, to art buyers, and clients to obtain a complete picture of what people in our industry are expecting from you right now.

I began developing the idea for this book because I believed that there is a need for an informative guide on this subject. However, while researching the book, I soon discovered that the level of expectation has risen so rapidly in the past few years that what was once viewed as acceptable only a short time ago is no longer competitive in the marketplace both on- and offline.

The growing competition in the industry, the advancement in digital technology, and the professionalism and dedication to portfolio in many of the schools and universities have in a matter of a few short years raised people's expectations toward portfolios.

Many creative professionals who are in the middle of their careers and considering changing jobs are stunned by the level of excellence of people many years their junior. The bar has risen and will continue to rise. If you wish to remain competitive in the marketplace, you need to be aware of what is happening all around you.

It also became apparent when talking to many creative professionals that the ones who are considered leaders in the industry have a strategy that others do not. Their insights are found in this book.

The *Breakthrough* *Portfolio* strategy

A breakthrough portfolio is not only a well-thought-out portfolio with some terrific samples of your work, it is a well-laid-out strategy of which your portfolio is an important piece but not the only piece.

The strategy consists of understanding who you are and who you want to become. It includes qualifying jobs and assignments and building a network of people who will be involved in helping you achieve your career goals. It will help you get to the type of work that you want to do and that you will be most successful doing.

In the following chapters I will be addressing these topics:

How to define your vision and communicate it to others

What is the real purpose of a portfolio

What to consider when building an online and offline portfolio

Where and how to looks for jobs

How to approach clients

The importance of follow up

What to do when you get the job

How to negotiate

What to do when things go bad

Where to find the resources that you need

Some tips from the pros

A portfolio should be original, fresh, and exciting, but that is not enough. It also needs to consider the audience. If you are an advertising art director, writer, photographer, or illustrator, each of your audiences will be expecting a different thing from you. Your work is about selling a product or a service, so no matter how great something looks or sounds, the great ideas combine creativity with a clear persuasive message. Your job is to persuade millions of consumers to try your client's products. For an artist working in three dimensions, like an architect, interior designer, automobile designer, or teapot designer you consider how well form marries function to solve the problem and how cost-effective the production is will become the criteria for how the work will be judged.

An environmental designer's process of arriving at a way-finding solution will be assessed on the clarity of the communication as well as the level of the graphic design. You were trained to solve problems, and you will be hired on your ability to show how your ideas solve problems. What was the challenge of the assignment and how insightful is your solution? If you are an editorial photographer, your photograph of an author should reveal something about the author, or it is just another snapshot.

Interviewers for jobs or assignments are very pragmatic. They are looking for someone to solve a very particular problem. If the person can bring additional skills to the company, even better but they must be able to solve the problem for which they are being interviewed. How you present the work and your selection of the work will be one of the determining factors in whether you will get the job. One story I hear repeatedly is that of individuals who present beautiful samples of work but no one can understand what the work is trying to communicate. Art directors seem to fall into this problem where the medium often overpowers the message. Remember your audience and what you are trying to communicate.

I know an art director who had one of the most beautiful books I had ever seen. The type, the page layout, the use of color and space were all beautiful; she is very gifted and desperately wanted to be an agency art director. She took me through a presentation of ads she had created. The layouts were beautiful but it was impossible to understand what products were being advertised. Her explanation was that she wanted to bring a new dialogue to the vocabulary of advertising. Sometimes type disappeared off the page or was heavily layered with type. It was beautiful to look at as art but the design was detrimental to the communication of the advertising message. I mentioned this to her, and suggested she

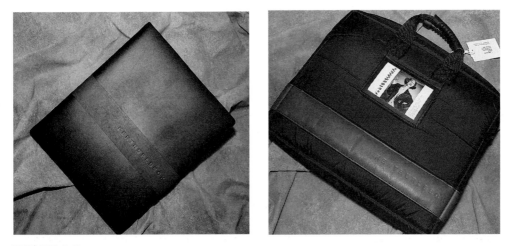

FIGURE 1.7

Sometimes a black portfolio is a practical way to go. I have a few portfolios that do a lot of traveling and get pretty beat up on the way. I have found a darker color keeps them looking better longer. In this case, I chose a black leather portfolio but to add personality I inserted a brown leather band, with my name embossed into it, wrapping around the cover. I also chose to apply the brown band on the black carrying case. This way when a client finishes looking at several portfolios, it is easy for him or her to identify and match up my carrying case and portfolio.

might have a better career experience working in a design house, but she had her heart set on being an advertising art director. I lost touch with her for a few years and finally bumped into her in Soho one day. I hardly recognized her with her huge wool cap, painted black leather jacket, and camouflage baggies.

She grabbed my arm and pulled out a portfolio out of her backpack. The whole thing was in a 5 × 7-inch metal box. Cool idea. After a couple of very frustrating years as an advertising art director she started designing some CD covers for a friend's small record company. Now she had a position with a major label doing some of their best bands. She hadn't compromised her work, she has just found the right venue that would appreciate the type of work she did. She is now recognized for the star that she is.

It goes both ways

Interviews are a wonderful opportunity to meet many different people with many different interviewing styles. While they will be assessing your ability to fit into their culture, the interview is also your chance to explore if they are the type of people with whom you want to work. Do they appreciate the type of work you do? Do they appreciate your personal style? Is this the right match? An interview doesn't only mean that they are there to check you out; it is equally important for you to find out who they are and whether or not you want to spend one third of your life with them. Do it nicely, but ask the questions and take the time to understand the people who you may be working with. You should leave an interview with a clear picture of whether you want the job, not solely with an idea that they might want you.

The eyes will be on you

Presenting your portfolio gives the interviewer a chance to assess your presentation skills. As a creative person, you will have the opportunity to present your work countless times throughout your career. It will be your job to sell the work that you created. And that doesn't mean talking nonstop though the presentation. It does mean creating an interesting, exciting journey. How you present yourself and your work can make the difference between selling your campaign and having another creative team selling their ideas.

Being a great presenter often entails being a great listener, too. Wallflowers do not end up being creative directors—great creatives with great presentation skills do. If you would rather have rusty nails shoved under your fingernails than stand up in front of a roomful of people to present your work, you have four choices if you want to succeed:

1. Get over it.

2. Find a position where you don't have to present.

3. Attach yourself to someone who is a great presenter

4. Get help and practice because you can do it.

There is more to creating a breakthrough presentation than collecting a few samples together

Remember your portfolio is your personal sales representative, it will open the door. But once open, it will be up to you to close the deal. It will be your responsibility to convince the interviewer that you are the magic behind the work you presented. The way you present yourself and your work are equally as important.

Here is a quick list of considerations; I will cover these in much more detail throughout the book.

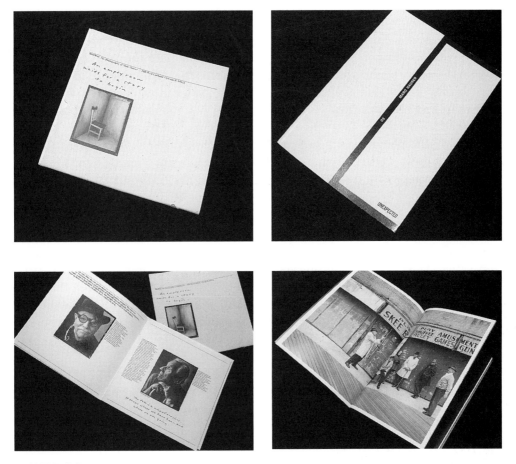

FIGURE 1.8

Photographer Marc Hauser creates portfolio books that he sends to his clients. The two that are shown here are titled "Stories" and "Unexpected." They are promotional pieces that will sit on his clients' shelves for a long time, continually reminding them about Marc. Marc's careful choice of subject matter combined with the right reproduction, paper, and layout make these books something to savor.

The don'ts

- Don't wait until the last minute to create your portfolio. Showing great work is not enough; you have to wow them with a great presentation.

- Don't ever show anybody's work but your own. It's a small, small world that we all work in. It might be a good idea but if it belongs to someone else it doesn't belong to you. This seems simple, but I can't tell you the number of times I have seen portfolios with other people's stuff in it, including work that I did. Believe me it's not a compliment to see work that you did in someone else's portfolio.

- Don't ever show anything you don't believe in 100%. I was just the (pick one, art director writer, photographer, illustrator, designer) and the (pick one, art director writer, photographer, illustrator, designer) was terrible but what I did was great. If you don't like it, fix it or don't show it.

- Don't put too many pieces in your portfolio. Your portfolio is judged by what you leave out as well as what you put into it. Your selection reflects directly on your creative judgment: 15 to 20 pieces are usually enough. It is always better having someone wanting to see more of what you have done than feeling that they have already seen too much.

- Don't assume that you will be with your portfolio every time it is presented. The presentation will have to speak for itself. If some work needs an explanation to be understood you will have to determine what type of explanation needs to accompany the work.

- Don't assume that everybody will like everything. You will meet a lot of people in your career and all will have an opinion. They don't necessarily have to agree with you.

FIGURE 1.9

The photographer for this book brought some antique block-printed Japanese green silk to The House of Portfolios. The results were a unique portfolio that is sure to separate him and his work from others and provide a story for the photographer to tell every time he presents his work.

- Don't apologize for your work. If you feel you have to apologize about a piece of work it shouldn't have been in there in the first place.

- Don't use puns. Arrrrrrrrrrrrrrrrrrrrggggggggggggggggghhhhhhhhh! Puns: No one likes them. Tell them to friends, but leave them out of the portfolio.

- Don't go to an interview with any preconceived ideas. Be open to what they may have to say. You may have gone in to talk about that position in Chicago working on the McDonald's account but they may have the Chanel account in Paris in mind for you.

The do's

- Do come prepared to listen.

- Do know to whom you are presenting your portfolio and know what they are looking for. Do arrive on time. They will probably make you wait but you shouldn't make them wait.

- Do shake hands when you meet your interviewer.

- Do have a resume

- Do present your resume, business card, or promotional card when you first meet.

- Do have a copy of your resume on the first inside page of your portfolio. The resume that you have given the interviewer is probably now sitting on their desk under your portfolio.

- Do be honest. They'll find out soon enough anyway if you're not.

- Do be very selective of the work you place in your portfolio. Even though it may be your favorite piece of work, there are times when it should not be included in your portfolio.

- Do respect the people you are showing your work to. Present your work properly.

- Do consider how to present your work. Just because it will fit into the paper envelope may not be the best reason to send it to a prospective client.

- Do show your portfolio and listen to what people say about it. You don't have to change anything, but it is always better to be informed than not.

- Do have a well-thought-out presentation with a beginning and an end. Be prepared to answer any questions about your work that you may be asked, from what was the strategy behind the work to who was the photographer.

- Do have confidence in your work. Not everyone will like everything, and that's okay.

- Do show your portfolio when it is ready, and not before. If you have thrown together a badly conceived portfolio, not only are you wasting your time and the time of the people you are presenting it to, you have also ruined your chances with that person for the future. You have one chance make sure everything is as good as you can make it.

- Do follow up EVERY meeting with a thank-you note. If you think that's old fashioned, then think of a creative way to follow up your appointment. The moment someone opens up your thank you may be right after they interviewed your competition. That's not a bad time to have them remember how much you impressed them.

- Do spell check everything.

- Do break any rule when there is a good reason to do so.

In summary

Creating a breakthrough portfolio is like writing a great symphony or creating a great film. You want people to remember more than the opening and closing credits. You want them to experience a great journey. The journey should create a memorable, exciting experience that says, "This is who I am, this is what I do and this is why you need me."

You will be judged not only on what they see but also on how well you orchestrate the journey. The more enjoyable and fun it is for you, the more it will be for them as well.

Your portfolio says, "Hey, this is who I am, this is what and how I think, and this is what I like." It is a statement on who you are. If you have an old beat-up case with work that has been tossed in at the last minute it says, "I don't care that much about you, and even less about myself."

Creating a truly breakthrough portfolio is about crafting a precision message that is powerful and single-minded. It is about making tough decisions. It separates and elevates. It takes a long career view.

FIGURE 1.10

When everyone was showing large portfolios, Marc Hauser went small. Marc's minibook contained more than 70 pages of samples of his work. But most important, the form this portfolio took was so unique that everyone who saw it wanted to talk to someone else about it. Sometimes you just have to break the rules.

Time to build some portfolios

You are going to build several portfolios. One to present to two different types of advertising agencies (one small creative boutique and the other a large international agency), one to a graphic design studio, one to a marketing department of a bank, and one to a recording company.

You don't have to actually put the work into a finished portfolio but simply collect it together in an ordered presentation.

The more specific you can make each of these companies the better your results will be. Which advertising agencies and which bank?

Now, decide for which type of job you want to build portfolios. You can make portfolios for an art director, graphic designer, illustrator, photographer, illustrator, architect, or copywriter. You can do portfolios for each one of them. You also will understand there are many ways to look at building a book. If you are a photographer, first do the assignment as an art director or vice versa.

Let's say you choose to make a portfolio for an art director. Gather samples of work that are not your own and that you feel would represent a good portfolio. You can gather samples from magazines or advertisements or CD covers or book covers–in fact, anything that you think could go into a portfolio. You will gather 15 to 20 samples of work for each of the companies for which you are creating a portfolio.

What you will need to consider

An advertising agency and a client is interested is seeing how well you understand their brand and how well you can sell their product or service. A creative boutique might want solutions that are edgy and unique whereas a large established agency might want solutions that, while unique also appeal to a broader audience. A recording company may want a solution that distinguishes their artists from other companies.

Does your portfolio communicate a vision? You will, as a potential client, be able to look through the portfolio and get an idea of the type of work that you do and your style.

The clearer the vision that you present, the easier it will be to communicate it to your potential client.

Place your finished portfolios on a table and look through them. How do they differ, and where are the similar. Is one stronger than the other? Could you use one portfolio to apply for several different jobs or would you need more than one.

Now write a couple of brief presentations for the portfolios. One presentation will be to the creative director, the other the account executive, and the other to the client. How would they differ? What is the important key message for each of these audiences?

The more you do this exercise, the better you will refine your skills at making objective decisions regarding the type of work that should go into a portfolio.

After you have completed this assignment put it aside and review it once again after you have finished this book. Would you now have done anything different in your presentation?

Creating your vision

STOP and take a deep breath, this is where your vision takes form

In this chapter you will learn how to separate your vision and presentation from all your competition. Reading the chapter, understanding it, and applying the principles will be one of the most important steps you will take in your career. No matter what level you are at in your career, you can take advantage of the information offered here.

This is a critical chapter for you because it will give you the tools to help you define your vision (or personal brand) and communicate it successfully to others. Some people do not like to apply the term *brand* to themselves, but whether you call it a brand, an image, or a vision they are interchangeable. The tools here, when, used correctly, will separate the major players from the minor ones.

These tools will help you communicate a clear picture of who *you* are and what *you* do. Who *you* are and how you do what *you* do are important because they make you distinct from your competition. As your reputation in the industry grows, the work that you produce will play an important role in communicating your vision. However as you begin your career it is critical to present a clear picture of yourself and the work that you are capable of producing.

Why this is important for you and your portfolio

A portfolio shows people the work that you have produced or the work that you are capable of doing. Right? Not exactly: There's more to it than that. A breakthrough portfolio reveals the clarity of your vision. *It reveals the clarity of your vision.* That is worth repeating because after someone has viewed your portfolio, you want him or her to have a positive memorable experience. No, more than that—you want to blow them off their chair with your vision. This is your moment to offer them an *experience* that differentiates your portfolio from others and get you the job. A potential client must experience and understand your vision. When they meet you or correspond with you, you want to continue to send out the same vision by keeping your message consistent.

If your portfolio only presents examples of the work that you have completed, it may not be the type of work that a potential client is looking for. If your portfolio presents a vision, the potential client will be able to see how it can be applied to any assignment he or she might have in mind.

FIGURE 2.1

Kristin Faulring moves easily between two- and three-dimensional assignments but the creative vision that she brings to each is very consistent.

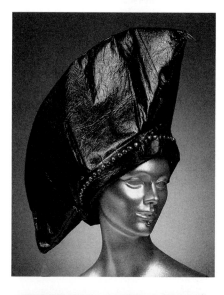

Your actions, your products, your communication, and your reputation define your vision, your brand, wherever you go. Whether you like it or not you will be defined. So you can either have others define who they think you are or you can present yourself to others in a way that you want them to see you. It's your choice. Now this may seem very, very obvious but the actions of people disprove that they understand this point.

If you are standing in front of a potential client or prospective employer explaining how meticulous your work habits are but your suit looks like it hasn't been ironed in 5 years or you hand him a crumbled resume, guess what? Your client will have a harder time believing you compared with someone who presents a well-groomed appearance or a crisp resume with the same story. Now both of you might be equally qualified but the one whose image is aligned to what he/she is saying will have the advantage. This is true whether you are a student looking for his/her first position or a professional looking to move up.

You make value judgments about the people you meet and work with, and guess what? They make judgments of you as well. People will make value judgments about the work you produce and how you produce it. People listen to what you say and see the work you produce then assess how what you say aligns with what you produce. Pretty soon a reputation is made and you have brand image. This is a good thing but only if you are the gatekeeper of your image.

Be who you is. Not who you ain't.
'Cause if you ain't who you is,
Then you is who you ain't.

Anonymous

Brand is experience

A brand is built through experiences. It comes from people's experience with you and the things you do. You can't build a brand without people experiencing it. A brand is built when what you tell people about what you deliver lives up to their experience (or doesn't) with whatever it is you delivered. If you tell someone that you are the world's best comedy copywriter of television commercials and they fall off a chair laughing after reading every script, you have delivered the experience that you promised. You have demonstrated your vision, or brand, and you have delivered it concretely.

Coca-Cola and others spend millions to ensure that they have the right brand image. In other words, they want to ensure that what they say about their product lives up to your experience with it. Whether drinking their product or watching a television commercial, Coke wants you to have an enjoyable experience with a quality product, and they deliver it.

Coke's brand is very different from Pepsi's, and loyal consumers of each would hotly dispute why one is better than the other. They are both sweet, carbonated, brown liquids but each has a clearly defined brand that came about through years of communicating a consistent message and delivering a product that lives up to the promise of the message.

Being able to clearly differentiate yourself from your competitors, the others that want the same job that you do, will help you to separate yourself from the pack and position you to succeed. And that is what we all want; so let's find out how to do it.

What are your defining attributes? Do you have any and why exactly do you need defining attributes?

First, yes you do have defining attributes, whether you want them or not, and as stated earlier, they are born from your actions. You want to ensure that the defining attributes that you are communicating are positive ones and important to whomever is giving out the assignments. If you could be a fly on the wall and listen to the way people describe you, it may not be the description that you would use for yourself. If you leave it up to happenstance, this inexactitude is surely what will happen. However, by clearly defining yourself and communicating this definition to others you will have a much better chance being viewed, as you would like others to see you. The choices that you make for your portfolio, business card, resume, and Web site and in fact every action, every decision, down to your choice of shoes, all communicate who you are, *your brand.*

I remember a story about Henry Ford that my father told me over breakfast one day—the Henry Ford who was the founder of the Ford motor company. Before Ford hired a top executive he would invite him to breakfast. If the executive salted his food before tasting it, Henry would not hire him. He believed that it showed an attribute of a person who performed an action without carefully considering the consequences. He wanted people with an attribute of being very circumspect in their decision process. It is important to know who you are talking to and what their expectations are. Hmmm... did I salt or not salt before I tasted my breakfast?

Not everyone you meet will like you or what you do. The more people you have supporting you and your ideas, the better your chances of success. Rarely will you find 100% of the people behind you 100% of the time. But you do want to build a support system where most of the people support you most of the time. You also want to put yourself in a position where your supporters have influence. That means aligning yourself with the people who have the power to get your ideas sold and who will pass the credit for coming up with the ideas back to you whether it's the company or client you work for.

Your vision will have to align with their vision to accomplish this. This complementarity is important to understand because the more clearly you define your vision and brand, the better your chances of finding similar thinking people. Later in this book I will address places where you might look to find these people.

John Lennon, a member of the music group, the Beatles once said, "Just when you think you know what's going to happen next, life happens." And he was right. Bad things happen to good people and bad alike. The creative industry is full of twists and turns, mergers, rapid downsizing, and rapid upsizing. You need a clear picture of yourself and how you align your vision to the overall workplace to have longevity in business.

As your career progresses there will be a shift in what will be expected from you and what you deliver. For example if one of your traits is that you work with and manage people well as you assume more responsibility and manage more people, you will emphasize this trait. Things are always changing which should be a good thing if you are ready to deal with the consequences of change.

FIGURE 2.2

Brian Ponto has a unique way of involving his audience. He designed an interactive portfolio; the portfolio was laminated and bound into a book. The viewer was challenged to interact with the book by actually writing comments or other contributions directly on the work with a set of markers that accompanied the portfolio. What does this say about Brian? It says he is a collaborator and that he thinks out of the box. (Courtesy of Brian Ponto; thesis instructor, Paul Sahre.)

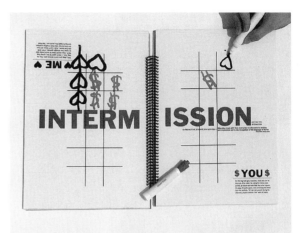

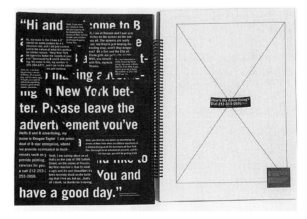

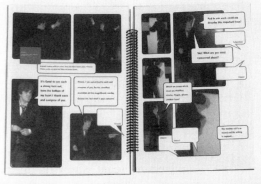

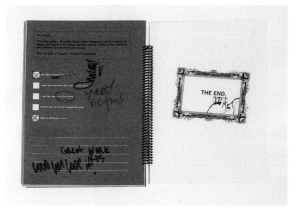

We are what we do

Let's say you decide to accept an assignment that does not hold your interest. You do a fine job, and the client accepts the work. Your friend accepts an assignment from the same company and he is thrilled to do it. Every time he talks to people at the company, they can feel his enthusiasm. He finishes the project and the client loves the work.

Next month, the client has another project. Who do you think they'll want to work with and what will they tell someone about their experience with you? You want to place yourself in positions that will foster success, which means, at the very least, showing interest in the work assigned to you or working on assignments that get you excited.

Think for a moment about some of the people you know. There are a variety of personalities and work ethics. Here are just a few. Do you recognize any of the following traits within yourself?

There are those who do the following:

- Miss or are always late with their assignments
- Never give credit to others
- Don't communicate well
- Are great collaborators
- Produce original and exciting work
- Produce sloppy uninspiring work
- You don't want to be in the same room with
- Are prone to being upset
- Are unreliable
- Always seem to get the best project
- Expect others to carry the weight

The list can continue for pages. Over time, people's traits, good and bad, become more pronounced to the people they work with. We are creatures of habit and generally find it easier not to change unless forced to. In addition the quality of the work that a person produces will define the ability of the person. Taken together their vision is defined, their brand is built. Now, everyone, *everyone*, wants to work with the people who are producing the best work and getting the most attention, but that doesn't always happen. To work with the best (i.e., a person who has built a strong reputation), this person has to want to work with you. You have to have value for that person. Another way of expressing it is that your values will have to align with the values of the person who approves the work. It doesn't mean you can't be creative and only give them what they expect. What it does mean is that they have a set of expectations and you have to meet or surpass those expectations.

If you were working on a project and had to choose five people to work with from the people you know who would you choose? If someone else had to do the same would you be one of the ones chosen? Do you have the defining attributes that make you the one others would choose to work with? Have you communicated those attributes in a way that would lead you to be chosen?

Defining your vision

Imagine yourself in a room full of people, half are art directors and half are people looking for art directors. You have about 30 seconds to meet and introduce yourself to as many people as you can. What would you say to convince them that you are the person who should get the assignment? In real life you usually do not get a full 30 seconds to grab someone's attention.

TIPS FROM THE PROS

"Art directors, writers, designers, they are all asked to work on many different types of accounts and need be versatile. However when I am looking at a portfolio I still need to get a sense of who that individual is. I need to look at the work and see something unique in this person's style."

Binnie Held
Held and Lloyd
Creative Recruiters

FIGURE 2.3

Drew Stalker brings a fresh approach to each assignment but the level of creativity he brings to each project is unmistakable. Drew's portfolio stands out because of the clarity of the ideas behind his concepts.

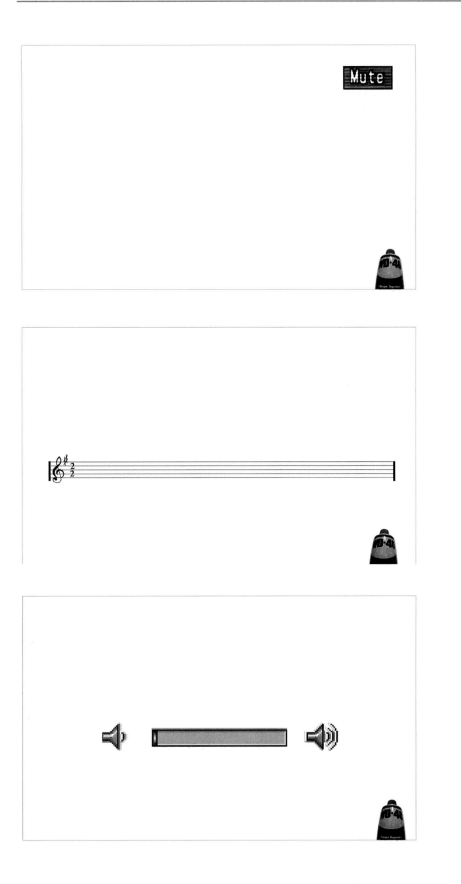

Okay, it's time to roll up your sleeves

You have 30 seconds to tell me who you are and why you should get an assignment. The dilemma is that there are 25 people who want it as much as you do and have more experience. If you decide to say that you would do a great job and would meet the deadline, you would say what everyone else would, too, most likely. How do you separate yourself from the pack? This is true whether you in New York, Los Angeles, London, or Milwaukee.

This is a situation you will face throughout your career. I have a presentation 2 days from now. There will be five companies pitching for the project. Two of the companies are considerably larger than mine, one smaller, and the fourth about the same size. We are all experts and all could accomplish the task, but when I leave the presentation I must convince this client that my company can bring more value than my competitors.

The way I will do this is by understanding their business and presenting my organization's attributes in a way that separates us from our competition and support the goals of the client.

This is what you are going to do now for yourself.

Its time to find out who you are

Wait a minute, after living with yourself for all these years you know exactly who you are. Right? Well yes, no, and maybe.

If you want to get somewhere you have to know how to get there. You need to have a good road map and know the capabilities of the vehicle that will take you there. This is where your trip begins.

There are two basic ways to look at working.

1. If I get this job or assignment I will be able to pay my rent.

2. If I get this job or assignment it will help me to bring my career to the next level, eventually making me important in my field, and my financial needs will be taken care of.

One of these basic perspectives is always applicable whichever level you are at in your career.

This book is about choices. The better the choices the stronger your career will be. It's your choice.

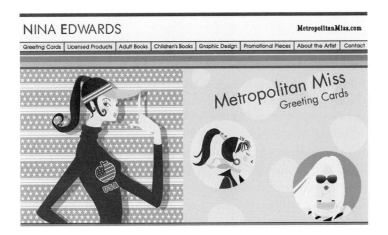

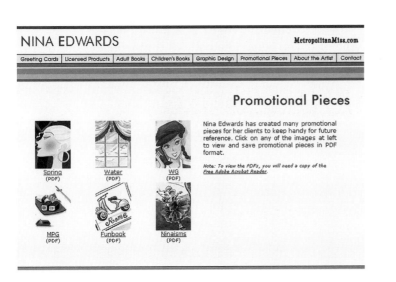

FIGURE 2.4

Sometimes it is the clarity of the presentation that makes it breakthrough as in the case of Nina Edwards' website. She presents a very clear picture of her services while showcasing her work at the same time. A visitor to her site is easily directed to the type of service for which they are looking to hire Nina, whether it's illustrations for adult books, greeting cards, licensing of images, or assignment work. The clarity of her vision is apparent on every page of her Web site.

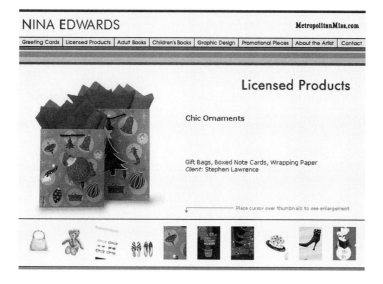

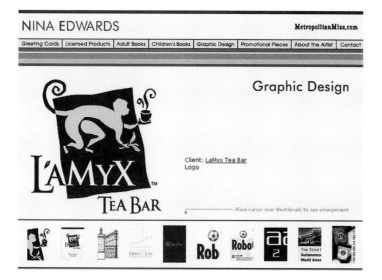

Creating the vision statement

Grab a big pad of paper because we are going to be dealing with some big ideas. Next sharpen up a dozen pencils. You can bring your colored ones, or magic markers if you want.

Start by selecting five sheets of paper. Each piece of paper will have one title as follows: 1. Underlying Values; 2. Distinguishing Values; 3. Tone and Expression; 4. Personality; and 5. Promise.

Place these pieces of paper on a table or tack them up on a wall with the paper titled "Underlying Values" on the bottom and the one titled "Promise" on the top.

These are the foundational blocks for building a brand or vision.

The Promise = What Do I Offer You.

Personality = What am I Like.

Tone/Expression = How Do I Present Myself.

Distinguishing Values = What Defines Me.

Underlying Values/

Core Values/Underlying Value = What Do I Need to Offer to be in this Business.

(The price of entry)

Now the fun begins.

Underlying values/core values

These are all the things that someone in your profession, in your category, doing the same kind of job you do, will need if he or she expects to get a job.

For example, let's look at the following professions
An art director should have the following:

- An understanding of and an interest in design and typography
- An understanding of basic graphic computer programs
- An ability to conceive ideas
- An ability to manage work flow
  An architect should have the following
- An understanding of and interest in three-dimensional design
- An appreciation of three-dimensional spaces
- An understanding of building standards and materials
  A writer should have the following:
- An understanding of grammar and writing structure
- An understanding of meter
- An ability to translate concepts into words
- An interest in communicating through words

A photographer should have the following:

- An understanding of film, cameras and lenses
- A degree of technical proficiency with his equipment
- A basic understanding of design
- An ability to take a correct exposure

A make-up artist should have the following:

- An understanding of skin types and face shapes
- An awareness of trends
- An ability to apply make-up

These are but a few examples. You should expand your own list by several points. If you cannot do so, take a step back and take a deep breath, sharpen your pencils, and get back to work. You should know the requirements that a person in your line of work needs to get a job in your field. If you are still stalling, this is a good point to stop and talk to some others who are working in your field. You want to make sure that you posses the necessary skills or have the interest to do the type of work you dream of doing.

Now, this may seem to be very elementary, but I have sat with people who are having problems in their job, and when we did this exercise, they have said, "You know, I never really wanted to do that."

Just because you might like to take photographs does not necessarily mean you should be a photographer. There are many other positions that are photo-related that you might be better suited from photo editors to photo stylists.

Distinguishing values: What defines me?

Next, move up to the next box, the one that you have titled "Distinguishing Values." Distinguishing valves are the things that differentiate you from every one else in your field of expertise. These are extremely helpful when you are looking for assignments. If you know what motivates you and what you do better than anyone else, it will be easier for you to communicate these things to someone else. It will help you get the assignment because you will be able to communicate how your expertise helps you solve their particular problem. These distinguishing values can be aspirational as well. You may want to include statements of values that you may not have perfected at the moment but that you are developing.

As you continue through the other boxes including personality and tone/expression you may discover other distinguishing values. So continue to revisit each of the boxes until you feel that you have exhausted your supply of descriptives.

Here are a few possible distinguishing values for art directors.

1. Able to quickly conceive very original and quirky solution

2. Able to have the patience to stick through long laborious detail oriented design solutions.

3. A powerful presenter and seller of ideas

4. Able to manage complicated projects.

5. Able to work well with others

   Here are a few you might choose for a designer.

1. Able to create unique solutions

2. Great sense of color and design

3. An innovator with typography

   There are dozens more, so add as many as you can to your list.

FIGURE 2.5

Photographer Rick Zalenski has been documenting found portraits for over two decades. The cover to his portfolio use a "Z" to indicate he is making his mark. The portfolio follows a format that is simply designed to focus maximum attention to his work and the subject matter.

Making your choice

Now, one art director might love to sit with an annual report for months specifying type for long complicated financial forms whereas another might find this to be the worst torture imaginable. If you are building your career, you want to make sure you know the type of projects on which you would like to work and the type of people you would like to surround yourself. If you like to be fast, on your feet moving from one project to the next, and that is how you do your best work, do not accept a position as an art director producing annual reports. You will not be producing your best work and you will build a reputation of someone who doesn't produce the type of work worthy of recognition.

Let's consider two examples of distinguishing values for a photographer:

Able to catch the action, no matter how fast it is moving.

Able to produce exquisitely crafted detailed images.

Action photographers, the type shooting sports or war photographs, have a split second to focus and capture a compelling image. They are looking for a moment in a situation where that one frame conveys the emotion of a larger event. A food photographer may spend a few hours placing and adjusting the lights while a group of food stylists coax a piece of lettuce in front of the camera to capture a beautifully detailed portrait of it. Putting a photographer who gets his adrenaline rush from standing on the 50-yard line with a 1000-mm lens in a studio to shoot a perfect strawberry shortcake would make him as unhappy as putting a food photographer on the 50-yard line in the rain during the Army-Navy game.

There are certain triggers that motivate you as a creative person. People often accept a creative assignment without thinking realistically about whether it is the right one for them. Sometimes, the right answer is "No, this is not the right assignment or job for me."

If you are doing what you do well and what you love to do will, over time, you will build a reputation for what you do. When someone has this type of project they will seek you out. This is how you build a cycle of success.

Tone/expression: How do I present myself?

Think of tone and expression as a suit. This is how you want others to perceive you. Are you an Armani, Donna Karan, or sweater-and-chinos kind of person? There is nothing wrong with being any of these types but if you are offered a position at a financial institution and are expected to come in daily in a three-piece suit when the farthest your willing to go fashion-wise is to tape a tie to your tee shirt, you may want to reconsider this position.

Your tone/expression box may fill up with any of the following descriptive words

Business-like

Corporate

Casual

Professional

Confident

Sophisticated

Fashionable

Avant-garde

Trendy

Conservative

Personality: What am I like?

This question should be interpreted in exactly the way it is written. In other words, think to yourself: How do I want people to see me? Your brand has to have a personality. A personality adds emotion and culture to a brand. Personality is a connecting element between you and your client.

Personality is what is inside you. Are you an introvert or extrovert: communicative, or not? What are the traits that you want to best describe yourself?

Introvert

Extrovert

Friendly

Outgoing

Shy

Quiet

Thoughtful

Humorous

Quirky

Flexible

Can you see what is beginning to take place? You are creating a professional profile. No two people will have identical profiles. Each is unique because everyone is unique. What is beginning to emerge is a profile that is unique to you with a set of words that describe who you are and what you do. As you move up to the top page in your stack of descriptive pages you will see that you have created a unique profile from which a unique promise will emerge. This profile will be the beginning of a statement that you will use to describe yourself to others.

Brand attributes

Brand Attributes are the indicators that help define your brand. They should be specific and differentiated. Here are some examples of brand attributes.

Innovation	Pioneer Spirit	Romantic
Sophistication	Beauty	Modern
Arrogance	Design	Safe
Confidence	Serious	Uniqueness
Openness	Friendly	Elegance
Technological	Fresh	Premium
Quality	Friendless	Sound
Urbane	Snobbishness	Advancement
Revolutionary	Power	Progressive
Quickness	Trustworthy	Strong
Sharp	Provocative	Impressive
Honest	Smart	Eminent

And these are but a few. How many more can you think of?

Time to review

Now, before moving on to your promise, or, what you have to offer, it is time to review and make some choices. Carefully look over the pages that you have completed. You should have a half a dozen to a dozen separate descriptors on each piece of paper. If you do not, spend a little more time and add some more. You can ask someone you work with or someone who knows you well to provide you with suggestions. If you have listed more that a dozen descriptors in each category, even better.

The next step is to eliminate all but five or six in each category. Choose the ones that are your strongest traits and that best describe you and the ones that you want to represent you. If you were having a hard time, this would be a good moment to ask someone who knows you well for his or her opinion.

When you have completed this assignment it is time to complete the final box, your promise.

Promise: What do I offer?

Your promise is what you have to offer that is truly different from what anyone else has to offer. When you look over the four pages that you have developed, you will see that you have created a profile that is unique to you.

Your promise will be developed from what you have written and your promise will be unique to you.

What you have been doing is building a profile that when sifted through, will help you communicate your vision. The next step is to compress these attributes into a statement that best describes who you are and what you do.

And this will make a difference. Consider the following promise or offering: Who would you rather give a job to?

Photographer 1
"Hello, I am a photographer, and I'd like to work for you."

Or

Photographer 2
"Hello, I am a photographer who shoots emotionally honest portraits because I am able to connect with my subjects in a way that allows me to reveal a insight into their personality.

You will probably be intrigued enough to want to know more about photographer number 2.

Now, it's your turn to sift though the work you did and come up with your own promise.

Testing your results

When you have arrived at your promise, it is time to put it to a test. There is no right or wrong answer, but there are sometimes better ones or ones that better represent you. Let's say your promise is to "Create dynamic leading edge fashion photographs," but you are introverted and do not enjoy interacting with people. Perhaps, rather than working with models, stylists, make-up artists, and so forth, you may want to choose another path doing still-life photography of fashion products for example.

As another example, imagine you are an art director who likes working with small business owners because you like to deliver solutions to people who can make decisions quickly, rather than working perhaps for a large agency where it may take months to create, sell, and produce a television commercial. Working in that environment would not be the right choice for you.

Look through what you have written about yourself. Often, you will find contradictions. This is good because this is exactly where you want to find them, on paper and before you are communicating your vision to others. This is a time to test and refine your vision.

Under "Personality" you may have listed yourself as an introvert but under "Defining Attributes" you may have said that you like to work with people.

Look through these pages carefully and make sure that your descriptors support one another from box to box. If you have a strong cohesive group of descriptors that support your promise, then you are ready to begin.

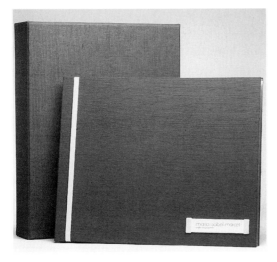

FIGURE 2.6

Maria Isabel Marcet has a presentation that is well thought out and has an impact. Her work is consistent and thoughtful, as is her presentation of the work. It is becoming more important to show that a creative person works outside of boundaries and can translate an idea through different types of media. Maria demonstrates this well in her portfolio.

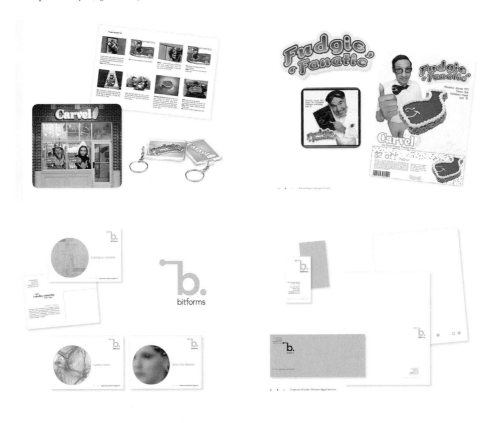

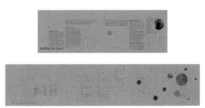

I thought this was about creating a portfolio?

Can you see what is happening here? You are creating a way that will describe you and your work. If you are positioning yourself to work in the banking business, shouldn't your portfolio look different from that if you were positioning yourself to work at MTV? Maybe your banking portfolio could be made from rich maroon leather whereas your portfolio for MTV might be covered in bubble wrap.

When you walk in a door, think about the signal that you want to send. You cannot be all things to all people. Understanding the differences of your audience is the first step to being successful.

In the following chapters, we will also apply what we have discovered here to your portfolios, resume, logo, business cards, and marketing material.

ASSIGNMENT 1

Find three people who you presently do not know and who are doing the type of work you want to do. Call and, if possible, meet with them and ask them to describe a typical week. Ask them about the tasks they perform, the skills they need, and the knowledge they must know to do what they do. Ask them how their job fits into their organization.

This works whether you are just starting out or trying to move up in your organization. For example, an art director may see his creative director every day and think he knows what he does; however, if the art director spoke to the boss he might find out that there are responsibilities that he'd never imagined.

What you want to understand is what it is like to be in their shoes and how the same position in a different organization might be similar or different.

What you also want to know is if this is the type of position that is right for you.

These first three contacts, as you will see later in the book, will be an important step for you to building a successful network.

Contact 1_____

Contact 2_____

Contact 3_____

You Are your hardest critic

Trying to be objective about you own work can often cause inertia. One day everything looks good, and the next day everything looks bad. Sometimes you don't feel there is any direction to where you are going. What can you do?

It's time to create an aspirational portfolio.

ASSIGNMENT 2

Swipe or aspirational portfolio and what can you gain by making one

In Chapter 1 you collected some work for different factious portfolios. Now you are going to collect work and build your dream portfolio. You will not be using your own work, rather you will collect work that you aspire to and wish you had done.

We all make choices, and these choices are different from the choices that other people make. An aspirational portfolio lets you step back and make decisions in a very objective environment. It can help you define your vision and strengths.

Here how it's done

Spend the next several days gathering examples of work that you love, respond to, and wish you had done—the kind you would want to represent you in your portfolio. Remember this is not work that you have created but work other people have done. Collect 40 to 50 samples. Look everywhere, in magazines, award books, other portfolios, and Web sites—anywhere you would expect to find great work. The bigger your selection, the better your results will be. Think of this time as a mini-vacation. All you should be doing is looking for the type of work you really enjoy and that makes you happy. Put no limitations on your search and selections.

Now, the hard part begins. Edit the 50 or so samples down to the best 30. Once you have done so ask yourself this question: "If I want to communicate my philosophy to someone, which pieces will do so the best?" Now hold that question in your mind as you edit down the 30 choices to the best 15 (i.e., those examples that would best communicate your vision). If you were to go out tomorrow to present your work for an assignment, this is the book that would best illustrate your thinking and the work you want to do. (One caution though: This is not your work so don't even think   about ever showing it as your work. This is an exercise to refine your vision and should be reserved for you alone.)

An interesting thing will begin to happen. We all make choices every day, and these choices help to form our ethics, personalities, preferences, and opinions. The work that you select for your aspirational portfolio will be different from the work another may choose. One illustrator may choose work that is very realistic whereas another may choose very interpretative work: Both works could be award winning.

But what should emerge from this exercise is a portfolio with a single, clear voice.

Now, place this portfolio next to yours and carefully look through the two. If these two portfolios were to be presented for the same assignment, which book would win the assignment? Does your portfolio communicate your vision as strongly as the other, and, if it doesn't, what can you do to eliminate the disparity?

Why this works.

1. This isn't your work so you can be more objective about your decisions.

2. It's aspirational. You are unlimited by budgets and so forth.

3. You will have chosen a coherent body of work.

4. You can do it at any point in your career and it will help you refine your own vision.

Let me give you an example. Gordon wrote comedy for advertising—great comedy. What was special about what he did was that he always found a situation that would reinforce the client's selling proposition. His punch lines always reinforced the client's message. He was the worst-dressed person in the agency and so notorious for being 45 minutes late that everyone always sent him a separate invitation to a meeting with a time 45 minutes before the actual scheduled starting time for the meeting. Then, he would only show up about 15 minutes late. He won awards for the agency and was pretty much left alone to create his brilliance. One day, out of the blue, Gordon walked into the creative director's office and resigned. Because of his visibility in the industry, he had been offered the job of a creative director with a large increase in salary and a group to manage on a very large piece of business for a financial institution. When questioned about this sudden change in career direction Gordon said that he had been in the business for a while and thought that it was time to take on a role with management potential; these words coming from a man who had a hard time managing to arrive at the agency before 11:00 every morning.

After about 3 months, Gordon was out of a job. The agency that hired him became increasingly unhappy with the work he was producing, and then he was disappointed by the work the client was buying. What was even worse was that because the newer work that was in his portfolio was of inferior quality, potential clients would now look at his portfolio and judge the work as inferior and question his role in the groundbreaking work that he had done at the agency where he previously worked.

What happened? Gordon lost sight of his defining attributes and how they fit into the world around him.

Reluctantly, he sat down and created a vision statement and then produced an aspirational portfolio. After he completed the portfolio, he returned to his vision statement and further refined it.

Looking at his vision statement, I felt that his distinguishing values were lacking. When I mentioned this to him, I remember he made a remark that made me break out laughing. He smiled and said, "Oh yeah." Then he added under distinguishing values: He could make anybody laugh. He was on his way to separating himself from his competition.

While he was creating his aspirational portfolio, he remembered just how much he enjoyed having fun with his work. He loved work that made him laugh and, above all, he loved creating work that made others laugh. He also liked having fun with his work.

He was embarrassed to return to the previous agency. But there is a happy ending: He bumped into his previous creative director and ended up returning to the agency. He now keeps a suit, shirt, and tie rolled up in his file cabinet for important client meetings and has two junior writers that he mentors. He is producing great work and he is happy. He still shows up late to meetings.

ASSIGNMENT 3

What makes you, you?

It is time to build your own vision statement and turn it into your own 30-second commercial. Take out the paper and get started. You want to end up with a clear picture of what you want to communicate to others about yourself.

This usually turns out to be a difficult assignment, but it shouldn't be one. If you built a solid vision statement, you already have a good start. You should have a good idea how to describe yourself and the work that you do. You should be able to communicate in 30 seconds who you are, what you do, and how who you are and what you do can benefit whoever has the job or assignment that you would like to clinch. Furthermore your description should clearly differentiate you from your competition.

You have a 30-second commercial about yourself–that works out to about 45 to 65 words. When you approach an assignment, you should make sure to discover what is wanted from you so you will know which of your attributes are important. Your 30-second commercial will be the backbone of your presentation but what you emphasize will depend upon the requirements of the assignment.

Try it out on friends and people who you meet. Does it sound like who you are? Are you comfortable being the person who you are describing? Write two or three or more if you need to, the idea is to be able to entice someone to want to know more about you. If you call someone on the telephone, 30 seconds may be all the time you get to make a connection.

Statement 1: _____

_____

Statement 2: _____

_____

Statement 3: _____

_____

Next we will look at your portfolio and marketing materials to ensure that they communicate the same message. This will include your resume; yes a resume is a marketing tool too.

CHAPTER 3

The Professional Portfolio

Picky, picky, picky, and you should be too

The professional portfolio vision makers share their secrets

I believe this is an important chapter because it gives you a glimpse into the workings of the people who developed the portfolio industry. It also shares some of their insights.

Whether or not you decide to make your own portfolio, buy one pre-made, or have one custom-made, there are always a few tips you can pick up from people who make professional custom portfolios for a living.

FIGURE 3.1

The folded portfolio box from Brewer Cantelmo.

They care about the work they do for you

The first thing you should know about the professional portfolio maker is that they approach every product with dedication, care, and excitement. They are in the business of contributing to a person's vision, and their expertise can raise the level of a person's presentation, helping him or her to blow open doors. They help contribute to the positioning of a professional in his or her marketplace. A person's professional standing is directly linked to how much he or she will earn and his or her visibility in the field.

A photographer placing an order for a dozen portfolios spent hours with Thomas Lombardo, the founder and president of The House of Portfolios. Thomas carefully reviewed dozens of cowhides to find the right ones for his portfolios. When the photographer was finally finished and ready to leave, the owner remembered a shipment of additional hides. He spent the time searching through every hide to make sure he found the ones that were the best matches in color and texture. He didn't have to do it, his client was happy with the first selection but Thomas wanted to make sure his client had the best possible choice. These craftsmen take deep pride in their products. They understand that the choices they make may encourage a potential art buyer to spend a little more time considering the work.

Making a portfolio is a craft. It requires precision and fine attention to detail. Every decision from the choosing of the material that will cover the book, to the number of pages it will contain, to its shape, size, color, and even the way the pages are bound, is discussed in detail. It is the intention of the professional portfolio builder to create a perfect portfolio, a work of art to hold your art. The balance here is to create an object of beauty and practicality that will enhance and compliment your work without overpowering it. It is like placing a beautiful frame around a beautiful painting. The right frame emphasizes the beauty of the art without drawing attention to itself. In doing so, it also contributes to the beauty of the presentation.

A beautiful portfolio does not have to cost a fortune, take your time to look around or consider building one.

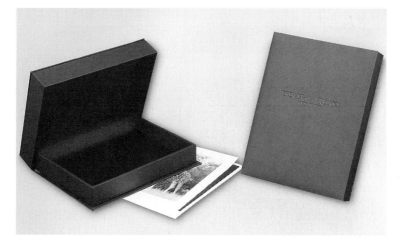

FIGURE 3.2

The Clam Shell from Brewer Cantelmo. This is a traditional design for displaying work mounted on boards.

Every decision, no matter how large or small, can contribute to your vision. Some choices will be subtle and may not be noticed at first glance by others; however, the choices will be recognized immediately to contributing to the overall look and feel of your presentation. Whether you want the cover of your portfolio with square edges or rounded edges may not seem like a very important decision, but if you are conveying a softer, more romantic image, rounded corners may be more appropriate. If, on the other hand, your work is very crisp, clean, and precise, squaring the corners on your portfolio may better support that vision. Then again, if you expect your portfolio to be on the road going from one presentation to another, rounded corners or reinforced corners should be a definite consideration.

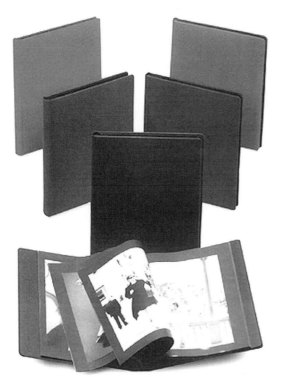

FIGURE 3.3

The Portfolio Book from The House of Portfolios. This is a handsome and versatile way to present your work. The work can be inserted into vinyl sleeves or printed on pages that can be fastened into the portfolio.

Decisions, decisions, decisions—what fun!

Materials should be selected for their durability and attractiveness. Choices of whether to use leather, cloth, wood, metal, or other material for the cover should be considered for the impact they have on the work and the impact on the prospective audience. There are a lot of choices and a lot of decisions.

These choices, if made well, will support your vision or *brand*. It will contribute to the overall experience when your work is reviewed. It can make the difference of someone quickly flipping though a portfolio or spending a longer time considering it.

The final decision as to which material to use is based on a number of decisions from what displays the work the best to what supports the image that you want to convey.

Once the decisions have been made as to the material, color, texture, size, whether it will be horizontal or vertical, whether it will it live in a box or clamshell, how many pages will be used, etc. Then whether, and if, you want your name printed or embossed or etched or attached to the cover of your portfolio is the final decision.

What does all this tell you? It tells you that there are people who really care about the appearance of their portfolio as much as you do. Think of them as your partners; ask them for their advice and ideas. They might be able to save you some money or present a unique solution that you may not have considered. The more you become aware of the level of competition in your field, the more you will pay attention to the details in your presentation. This book gives you a head start by providing you with insights into the decision process.

Buying a book off the shelf: What you should know

If you make the decision to buy a pre-made portfolio from an art store or manufacturer, you want to make certain that you consider beforehand what you expect from it and how you want to display your work. You need to choose a portfolio that works for you, rather than finding a portfolio that will require you to reshape your work to fit its style. There are some great off-the-shelf portfolios available, but what counts is what you do with it to make it yours.

FIGURE 3.4

The Presentation Mailer with handle from The House of Portfolios.

An important decision when you are buying a pre-made portfolio is to select one that is physically perfect. Portfolios will become damaged over time. Although most people are respectful of another's portfolio, they do get stacked in corners, dropped, bashed, banged, and bruised. When choosing a portfolio, start with the one in the best condition you can find—as long as you settle for perfect condition. When you find the one you want, look at it carefully. If it has been sitting on the rack, other shoppers have pushed and prodded it. Open it up. If it has vinyl pages, are the pages in good condition? Does it have the number of pages that you need? Can pages be easily added or deleted? Are the metal rings that bind pages in perfect shape (these are the things that bend out of shape easily that could damage your pages)? If you are looking for a clamshell portfolio, check to ensure the corners are in perfect shape and that the spine opens evenly. Is the cover discolored? If you are looking at a portfolio that has been sitting on display, ask if they have one that is still in the box from the manufacturer. Remember, you want to start from the best place possible. Then anything you decide to add to the portfolio is your choice. If you want to give the portfolio an urban street look, then make it your decision where you want the tears and how they look. If you are working on a tight budget, look for somewhere else to save. Your portfolio is *that* important.

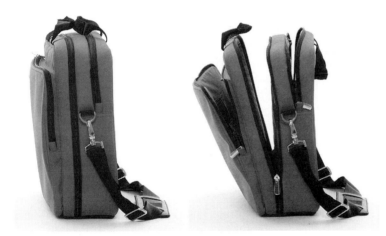

FIGURE 3.5

Here is an interesting solution from Casauri. This is a multipocket case that can hold a portfolio and computer in case you want to show a presentation from your computer. There is also a matching case for your iPod. Many photographers are using iPods to show additional work to their clients.

FIGURE 3.6

A selection of portfolio covers from Brewer Cantelmo.

The damaged portfolio that is sitting in the corner with a discounted price tag on it should be left sitting in the corner. Everyone has a budget, even someone spending several hundred dollars on a custom portfolio. However, you should start with the best one that you can afford.

The argument that the portfolio over time will become banged and bruised is not a good reason to buy one that is already damaged. In fact, the time when your portfolio begins to show its age is the time to replace it.

Although it might seem excessive to concentrate this much on the details, there are people who design and build the perfect custom portfolio—you are in competition with those people. Every day the custom builders are looking for better and more unique materials and better ways to construct their portfolios. They realize that you are in a very competitive business, and they are a part of it as well.

If you make the decision to buy a pre-made portfolio, visit or log on to the Web site of a custom

> ## TIPS FROM THE PROS
>
> "I think people are craving something very original...They're tired of the same old thing, so I love being able to create something that is exclusively for them. I like to juxtapose different eras, like fusing very classic, refined design with some of the street-smart energy of present-day fashion. I make sure that each product meets with unanimous appreciation in both form and function."
>
> *Jason Brown*
> *President*
> *Lost Luggage*

FIGURE 3.7

A selection of portfolio of Cordura/nylon carrying cases from The House of Portfolios.

portfolio maker. Often, generic custom made portfolios are very affordable. Take a good look at all the options that are available to you before you commit to buying your portfolio. The resource section in the back of this book is a good starting point to begin your search. A couple of hours visiting these companies on the Internet or in person should provide you with a plethora of ideas and a wealth of inspiration.

Booking on the custom portfolio manufacturer

You will realize early in your relationship that custom portfolio houses care as much about the look of your portfolio as you do. Your complete presentation makes a statement about you, and their portfolios make a statement about them. The better the portfolio maker, the more questions they will ask.

Although it is good to have an idea about what you want your portfolio to look like, it is a good idea to keep an open mind when visiting a custom portfolio manufacturer. They make a lot of different products and see even more. They are always looking for fresh ideas that will help their clients produce outstanding books. Their suggestions might add a detail that will separate your portfolio from the others.

It is important to discuss what the portfolio will look like as well as how it will be used. The choice of leather may give the portfolio a professional look, but if it is expected to do a lot of traveling, a man-made material may be a better choice.

It is a good idea to have a clear vision of the image that you want to convey and communicate that vision to the portfolio house. Warm, soft, hard, contemporary, or

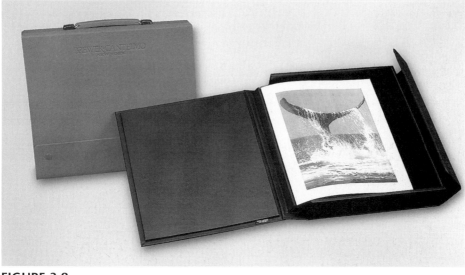

FIGURE 3.8

The Presentation Case with handle from Brewer Cantelmo.

traditional—the more descriptors you can provide them, the better they will be able to guide you to a unique and personalized solution that reflects your brand.

Portfolio manufacturers have a large selection of materials to choose from and welcome the discussion of new materials that you might have discovered. Chances are that they have had experience with it and can provide you with an educated opinion as to what it would look like on a finished book and how well it will stand up over time.

Even the page protectors can influence the look and feel of you presentation. If you decide to go this route, bring some of your work and try out different page protectors. Can you change the work easily without damaging the protector or backing? Is it durable? Is the vinyl highly reflective and if so, does it interfere with the viewing of the work? How does it feel? Is it possible to change the mounting paper so you can choose you own colored paper? All of these can influence the viewer.

Portfolio craftsmen can also make you aware of the latest trends and products or issues that you may have never considered yourself. If you will be sending your portfolio to other locations how will you protect it? How will it be sent? If you will be sending it often, it probably is good idea to have it sized so it will fit in one of the standard mailing boxes you will find at FedEx, UPS, or the post office.

A large portfolio can look impressive, but if you are sending it out on a regular basis and are expected to pay the shipping it may be more economical for you to produce a smaller one. If shipping will be a concern it is a good idea to mock up a sample portfolio and take it to the post office or FedEx and get a shipping quote.

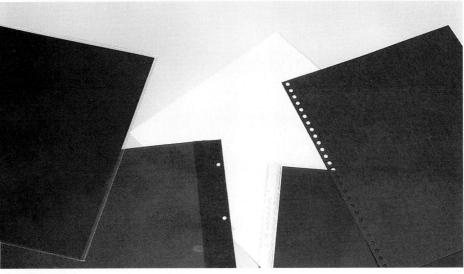

FIGURE 3.9

A selection of sheet protectors from Brewer Cantelmo.

FIGURE 3.10

The Presentation Box from Brewer Cantelmo.

A custom portfolio manufacturer tour

Custom portfolios are made by hand and the following tour at The House of Portfolios in New York will give you an insight into the care and detail that goes into their creation. Every step is carefully considered and the attention to detail is of the highest standard. You can look for ideas that might apply to your own portfolio should you decide to build one.

FIGURE 3.11

Custom portfolio makers will have on hand a wide selection of material from which to choose from. Your choices can include fabric, leather, vinyl, rubber, or your own material. They will be ready to help you with what ever you have in mind. (Figure courtesy of the House of Portfolios. Photo by David Mandel.)

FIGURE 3.12

Once the material is chosen, a quantity is carefully selected and cut to ensure that all the portfolios in your order will look consistent. This means making sure that the grain or pattern in the material is free from flaws and that the each piece of material is identical in quality. (Figure courtesy of the House of Portfolios. Photo by David Mandel.)

FIGURE 3.13

The portfolio begins as a piece of crushed board. After the board is covered with an even coat of adhesive, it is ready to accept the cover material. (Figure courtesy of the House of Portfolios. Photo by David Mandel.)

FIGURE 3.14

The final preparations to the board are addressed before the cover material is applied. (Figure courtesy of the House of Portfolios. Photo by David Mandel.)

FIGURE 3.15

Each step is carefully considered. After the outside cover is applied, the edges are glued and folded inside the cover leaf. (Figure courtesy of the House of Portfolios. Photo by David Mandel.)

FIGURE 3.16

The inside edges are trimmed of excess material. (Figure courtesy of the House of Portfolios. Photo by David Mandel.)

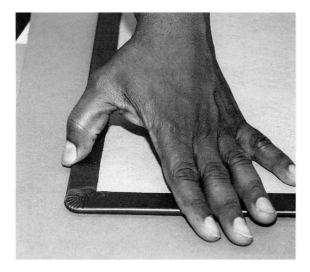

FIGURE 3.17

The edges are flattened in preparation for the inside lining. This is demonstrated on a portfolio that will have round edges. You can choose round or square edges depending on the effect you desire. (Figure courtesy of the House of Portfolios. Photo by David Mandel.)

FIGURE 3.18

With the outside corners attached the portfolio begins to take shape. (Figure courtesy of the House of Portfolios. Photo by David Mandel.)

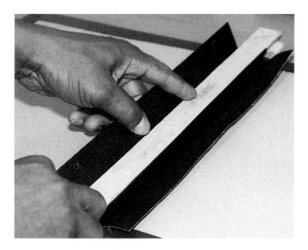

FIGURE 3.19

Next, the inner spine gets attention. It is important that the spine fit perfectly because the way the pages fit will depend upon how well the spine is positioned. (Figure courtesy of the House of Portfolios. Photo by David Mandel.)

FIGURE 3.20

There are inspections at every step of the way. If at any of these inspections the work does not meet their standard of excellence, it does not proceed to the next step. (Figure courtesy of the House of Portfolios. Photo by David Mandel.)

FIGURE 3.21

When the outside cover meets approval, the inside covers are prepared. (Figure courtesy of the House of Portfolios. Photo by David Mandel.)

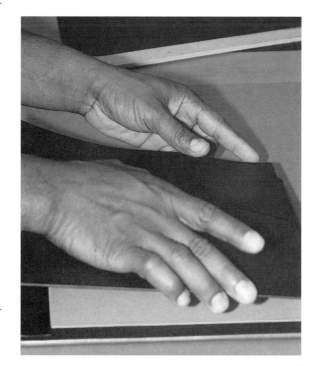

FIGURE 3.22

Almost there! The inside covers get their final touches. (Figure courtesy of the House of Portfolios. Photo by David Mandel.)

FIGURE 3.23

The portfolio is placed in a press to ensure evenness to the final result. (Figure courtesy of the House of Portfolios. Photo by David Mandel.)

FIGURE 3.24

The final book heads to the inspection station again. (Figure courtesy of the House of Portfolios. Photo by David Mandel.)

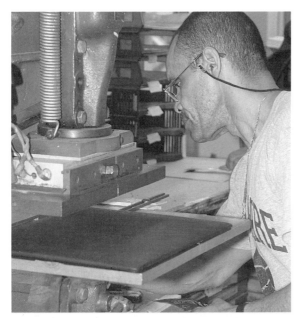

FIGURE 3.25

Some people like to have their names embossed on the cover of the portfolio. This is done by hand. It can personalize the portfolio and add a nice professional touch. Once this is done it is ready for your work. (Figure courtesy of the House of Portfolios. Photo by David Mandel.)

FIGURE 3.26

The Slim Folio from The House of Portfolios.

Your choice

A custom portfolio might have a longer life and be more distinctive than one that is bought off the shelf. It will definitely be designed to accommodate your needs without compromise. The more customization you want, the higher the price. Even if you purchase a production model or off-the-shelf generic one from a custom manufacturer, if you decide to emboss your name on the front you will pay for the service, but it might be a very nice touch to the portfolio.

The process of working with a custom builder may take several weeks, so plan ahead, and don't leave it to the last minute.

Tips from the people doing this for a living: Shipping your portfolio

When sending or shipping your portfolio, it is a good idea to seal it in two ziplock plastic bags. It may be bright and sunny the day it leaves on its journey, but many things can happen to a parcel on its way to its final destination. This includes packages sent through the mail or messenger services or even a delivery that you personally make. Things can happen to your portfolio: Someone can spill their coffee on it, someone can leave it sitting on the tarmac at an airport during a rainstorm while other packages are being loaded onto an airplane, or another package can leak and spoil your work if it is not properly sealed. It happens every day, and it could happen to your work. The rule here is whatever can go wrong will, so be prepared for whatever might happen.

You may have written the destination and your return very clearly on the outside of the shipping container, but what happens if the package is damaged? What if the mailroom opens the package and loses the shipping information? The destination of the package and your return contact information should be clearly marked on the inside of the package as well.

FIGURE 3.27

The House of Portfolios' Flap Folio book.

Not only are you protecting your portfolio and the work contained in it, you are also sending the message that your portfolio is important. It makes you look professional, and if you show others that you are careful with your work, they are more likely to be careful with it as well.

The drop-off receipt

You've rushed to drop your portfolio for a potential opportunity. Not hearing from the company after a few days, you call to check on its status.

> *Your portfolio? No, we never received it.*

What do you do now? If you have a portfolio receipt, you will have a chance to find where it is; if not, you are on our own.

This falls in the category of *things to do to make my life easier.*

The portfolio receipt is a very simple way of keeping track of where your portfolio is. If you have more than one portfolio, it even becomes more important. When using a shipping service like FedEx or the post office you can track your shipment. You might even consider using these services in the city where you live if there is not a good local courier or messenger service. Whenever you can, use the portfolio receipt like the one described in the following sections. It makes the recipient aware that he or she is responsible for receiving the package and helps you keep track of where your portfolio has been sent.

Here is an example of a simple portfolio request form.

From: *Your Name, Address, Telephone and E-Mail*

Portfolio Receipt

Delivered to: *Name*

Address: _____

Telephone: _____

Return instructions: Portfolio to be picked up by photographer after notification

from: *Recipient's Name*

This portfolio is delivered for examination only. Recipient assumes all risk for prepaid return of undamaged portfolio by the means and manner indicated above. A description of the portfolio, its contents and their agreed upon value for the purpose of liquidating any damage or loss is listed below. Please Handle with Care.

○ ○

DESCRIPTION OF CONTENT

1 Custom Portfolio Case

23 bound pages with photographs

1 Carrying case

○ ○

Minimum Value of Portfolio contents including portfolio and carrying case:

$ 0000.00

Portfolio contents including works may not be reproduced, copied, projected, televised, digitized, or used in any way without (a) express permission on Owner's invoice stating rights licensed and the terms thereof and (b) payment of said invoice. The reasonable and stipulated fee for unauthorized use shall be (3x) Owner's normal fee for such usage. Client assumes insurer's liability for all portfolio material.

RECEIVED BY:_____
                              Signature   Print Name

DATE: _____

Form: Portfolio Receipt Copyright 2003 Thurlbeck Studio

And, in summary...

Your portfolio is your ambassador. It is your voice. It will open doors for you. Take the time to do your research well before you need it. There are dozens of choices to explore; choices that will help you make a statement that best represents who you are. Don't stop looking until you have made the portfolio the best that you can.

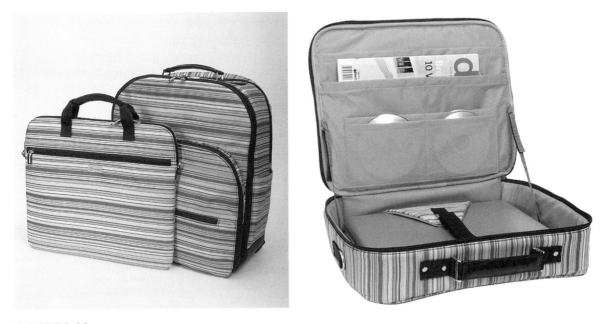

FIGURE 3.28

Casauri has come up with a clever solution for a carrying case that holds a portfolio or computer, CDs, promotional cards, and resumes encased in a lively eye-grabbing fabric.

YOUR ASSIGNMENT

Tailor your portfolio to your presentation

This is the time to start thinking about what type of portfolio is suited to your presentation.

A list of resources is provided in the back of this book. You can visit most of these companies online or in person. Look at what these companies offer, talk to the people who work there, and have them share their ideas with you. Visit these companies online and get an understanding of the types of looks and feel of the portfolios that they have to offer. It is time to start thinking about how you might want to present your own work by developing your own portfolio source book.

Download images from the portfolio sites and collect them into an idea book. Visit a fabric or plastics store and collect samples of material that inspires you. You can do sketches, like the ones below, and apply fabrics to give you an idea of the possibilities that exist. Some great resources can be found at art stores in their paper divisions or hardware stores in their wood veneer, vinyl adhesive, or wallpaper aisles.

FIGURE 3.29

Draw your own or use these portfolios on these pages and apply different surfaces to it. Where and how would you apply your name or logo? Try a dozen or more and compare. Do they stand out? Which one is sending the message that you want to deliver?

Making the Portfolio

QUOTE

"I was talking to one of my students, a very talent[ed] graphic designer. She dressed in a total black outfit with lots of straps and tears, with hair that looked as if it was exploding. She had piercings in her ears, nose, lips, cheeks and I was sure other places that would be interesting conversation topics.

She was graduating with a strong portfolio and when I asked her if she had thought of what kind of companies she was going to target. She must have registered the surprise on my face when she mentioned she wanted to work with financial firms.

"Oh the piercings, hair, like the style," she said, "yeah, they're gonna go. This is my school look." She knew it, but many do not. You have to know your market and what they expect. Never let your appearance outshine your portfolio. They are hiring you because of your work not how creatively you dress."

Susan Coutler-Block
Chairperson
Communication Design
Fashion Institute of Technology, New York

This chapter will offer advice on assembling your portfolio and interpreting your vision into a visual language that is consistent with your brand. First, the last thing you want is someone to remember the portfolio and not the work inside it, and last, you want someone to be moved by an unforgettable experience.

In the marketplace, you are judged on your overall presentation. Although it may be true that it is all about the work in the portfolio, when you are competing in the marketplace you need to keep in mind that you will be competing with others who are presenting equally strong work samples. Some will probably even be stronger.

The consistency and quality of the whole presentation, including your follow up, will make an impression. A little extra effort may be all the difference that it takes to grab someone's attention and separate you from others in the pack.

FIGURE 4.1

A portfolio with a wood cover from
www.Lost-Luggage.com.

There is a balance

Tom is an illustrator with a vision. Facing fierce competition, he wanted to set his presentation apart from every one else's. One weekend while he was helping his dad build a home bar, Tom discovered a beautiful exotic wood panel veneer that his father intended to use to cover the bar. Commonly known as zebra wood, it is a wood that had a pronounced light-and-dark–striped pattern running through it. It is a nice-looking wood.

This gave Tom an idea. Over the next few weeks, he worked long hours, days, and nights creating an outstanding portfolio. He spent hours drawing up the plans—even thinking ahead to ensure it would easily slip into the back seat of his Volkswagen. The portfolio was designed to reveal upon opening an easel-type presentation where his work would be hinged and present itself at a 45-degree angle to the viewer. During the construction, Tom realized that the wood and frame was adding substantial weight so he added wheels and a folding stand that would spring open at desk height with a simple flick of the wrist.

The presentation box was finished with polished brass hardware. The wood was hand polished with a Swedish wood-rubbing compound. The work was meticulously mounted and an etched brass plate with his logo, name, and Web site address was flush mounted on the outside of the box. It was a work of art.

He dropped the portfolio off with the art buyer of a large agency and was pleasantly surprised to find a message on his answering machine from the art

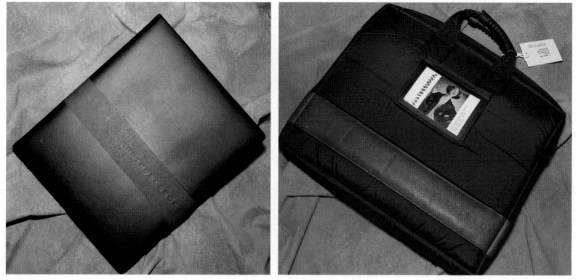

PLATE 1.

Here is a way to add a little differentiation to a black portfolio. In this case a brown bar carrying an embossed name was added to create a distinctive signature to the presentation. An additional advantage of this technique will come when the clients have looked through a dozen portfolios and begin to put them back in their respective carrying cases. A portfolio that has some design that is reflected in the carrying case is a better guarantee that you will get back the same portfolio and carrying case that you initially set to the client.

PLATE 2.

A few of Marc Hauser's promotional books.

PLATE 3.

Here a photographer used antique block-printed Japanese silk to cover a portfolio.

PLATE 4.

Rick Zalenski's portfolio and images. Each image captures a split second that tells a story.

PLATE 5.

Martin Kellersmann has a very unique vision. He has found that upon first viewing many people have a lot of questions about the work and his technique behind it. Martin has included a explanation of his approach to accompany the portfolio.

PLATE 6.

A portfolio is a living creation. In Chapter 6 one of photographer Tom McGhee's websites is displayed. During the writing of this book he further evolved his site updating it with new work. Although the new site is a has a different design the vision of the site remains consistent with his brand.

PLATE 7.

Chie Ushio's promo pieces not only catch attention but they get the right response.

PLATE 8.

Zave Smith has done a wonderful job of keeping a consistency and freshness throughout his marketing effort.

PLATE 9.

Anne Liu, a former Miss Asia, is an artist who uses herself as her canvas. She does photographs of herself representing different types of Asian women.

PLATE 10.

Paul Mathew Wood's self promo immediately caught my attention and has become very viral. Everyone who I describe it to wants to see it.

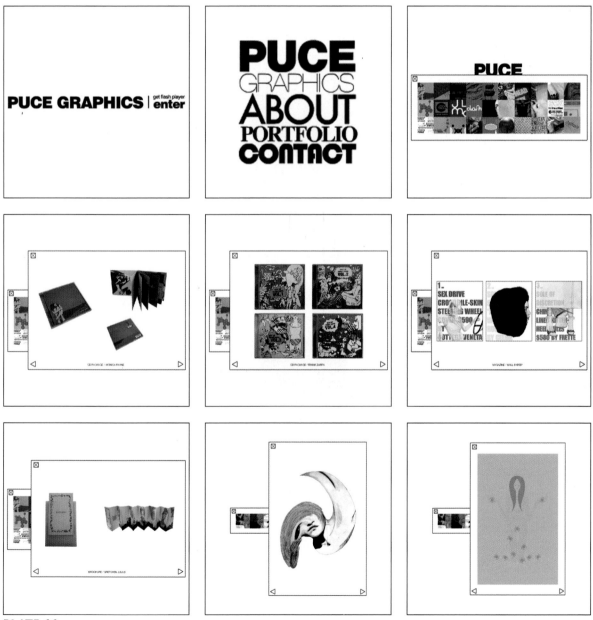

PLATE 11.

Puce Graphics have produced a website with a very simple but very engaging navigational system to guide the user through the portfolio.

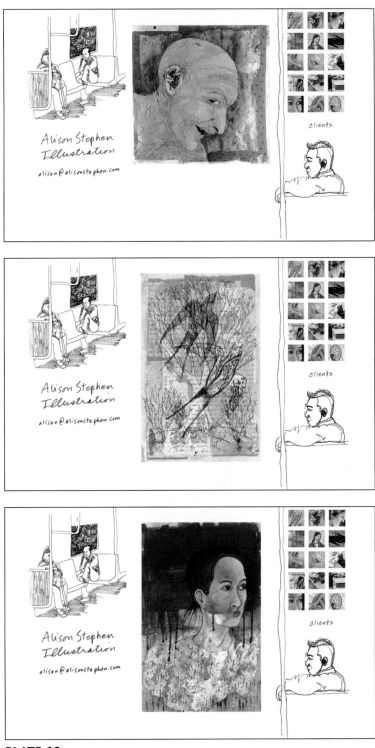

PLATE 12.

Alison Stephen's website is simple and elegant, perfectly reflecting her own style.

PLATE 13.

Patrick Dorian wants to engage and entertain you and certainly does with his website.

PLATE 14.

Leela Corman has created a journey with her acerbic story
telling. The rhythm of her site is created by her cleverly hiding
a surprise around each corner.

PLATE 15.

I like to make a statement about the work that a viewer is about to see. Here is a cover for one of my portrait portfolios with a few of the photographs.

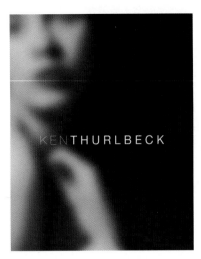

KEN THURLBECK

PLATE 16.

Here is one of my fashion beauty portfolios. Although the narrative of the work is different from the portrait book the branding and basic vocabulary of the work speak with a singular voice and brand.

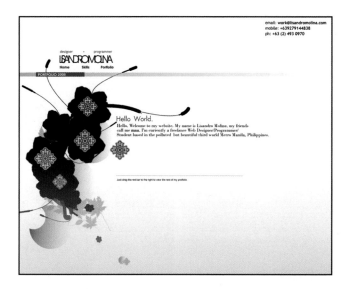

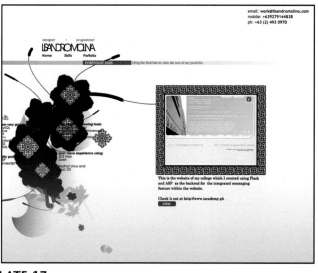

PLATE 17.

Lisandro Molina's site centers around a playful navigation system.

PLATE 18.

Frank Veronsky has done pretty much the opposite of most people. His website is more of an experience than a portfolio with navigation. But it succeeds because it engages the viewer

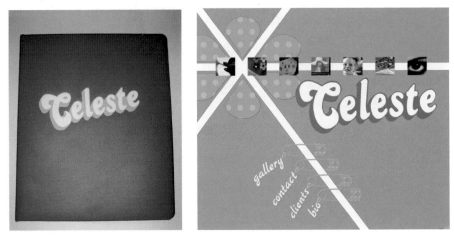

PLATE 19.

Celeste Calino's work is fresh and edgy. Here is the cover of her portfolio and a couple of pages from her website. They work together perfectly.

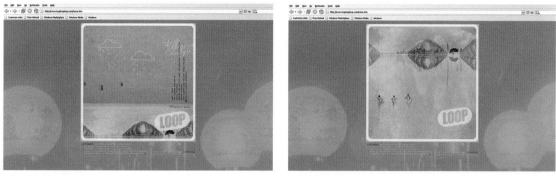

PLATE 20.

Tanda Francis is a designer making quite a name for herself in the international market.

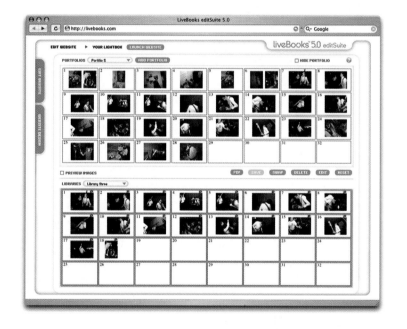

PLATE 21.

Michael Custuros was frustrated by the solutions that existed for building online portfolios. He started Livebooks.com. The LiveBooks is a web-based Flash website/edit Suite solution. His company offers a Lite Site, Pro Site and a student site at Livebooksedu.com.

I have included 4 examples of working sites that use this tool. (Lyle Owerko, Maki Kawakita, Colin Finlay, and Ken Thurlbeck) After much research Michael developed a system that has answered the needs of the community. What he has done is important enough to show 4 examples of his product because he has built a simple framework that allow his clients to easily build, launch and update a branded website

Notice while the basic format of each site follows a similar structure each photographer is speaking clearly with his/her own voice. The sites load quickly and present the work in a maximum size and resolution for the web. Although 4 photography sites are shown here this product can work for art directors, designers illustrators—in fact anyone showing images of their work.

PLATE 22.

Lyle Owerko.

PLATE 23.

Maki Kawakita. Livebooks has a feature shown here where a special password-protected page can be added. This allows Maki to share work with her clients online. A great feature for reviewing work or presenting custom portfolios to a client.

PLATE 24.

Colin Finlay.

PLATE 25.

Ken Thurlbeck.

PLATE 26.

Here is my company's site for radical media. Although the type of work is different from my photography site the branding is consistent and reflects a singular voice.

MAKING THE PORTFOLIO 79

buyer when he arrived back to his studio. She sounded very excited, saying that the creative director of the agency wanted to see him immediately there was a major presentation to a new client and they wanted to enlist Tom's talent.

It was the break he was looking for and Tom felt that all his time an effort paid off. He jumped back into his Volkswagen and headed back to the agency.

When he arrived, he was immediately ushered in to the creative director's office where he found a small crowd flipping through his work. Tom was introduced to the president of the agency and vice president account director. All were extremely impressed with the presentation. "Where did he ever find this presentation case?" 'they asked.

Tom told them the story of helping his father build a bar and getting the idea to use the material for his own presentation. "This was exactly what the agency needed," said the president, adding, "And how unique building it on wheels. It would be easy to roll from conference room to conference room for presentation. How much to build five?"

This was not exactly what Tom wanted to hear. When he was alone with the creative director he asked about the job he had submitted his work for and was told it wasn't exactly right for the project but they were happy to give him a contract for building several portfolios for the agency.

There are some amazing portfolios out there, so amazing that they dwarf the contents that are inside them. There is a balance. The portfolio should be like a trailer for a movie. It should give the viewer a clue that he or she is about to experience something very incredible, very exciting—your work—but the book itself shouldn't be the show. If you have a truly outstanding portfolio case, make certain that you have truly outstanding work inside of it. In fact if you were to interview the people handing out the jobs, as I have done, they would be unanimous in saying that it is all about the work. Regardless, time after time again someone would pull out a breakthrough portfolio and say, "Hold on a minute! I got to show your work to someone who has something that would be right for you."

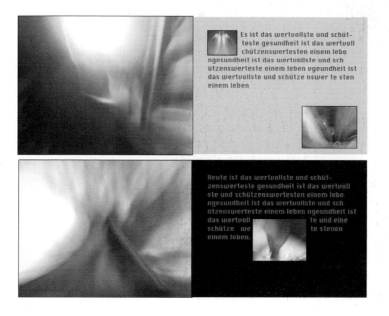

FIGURE 4.2

Martin Kellersmann, an artist living in Düsseldorf, has developed a unique technique for his photography. Using a digital camera his *dances with camera* style presents a vision that separates him from other photographers. Because his vision is a radical departure from most photographers' style, he introduced his portfolio with an artist's statement and explanation of his technique.

I was speaking to a photo editor about the variety of portfolios he saw. He mentioned that he is constantly amazed at the material people use to cover their portfolios. He saw one that was covered with very long hair. When he asked the artist why he did it, the reply was, "because it's cool." The art buyer's response was that he didn't think it was cool at all because it didn't have anything to do with the work.

Sometimes you have to listen.

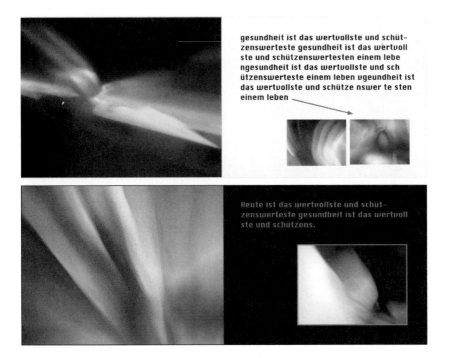

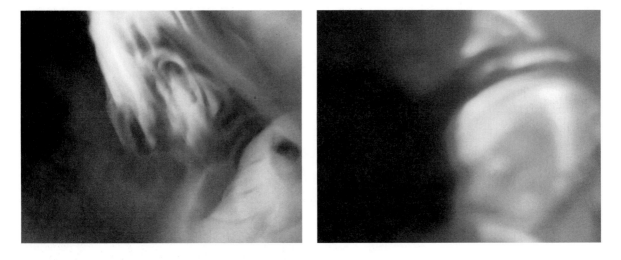

FIGURE 4.3

Some examples of Martin Kellersmann's photographs.

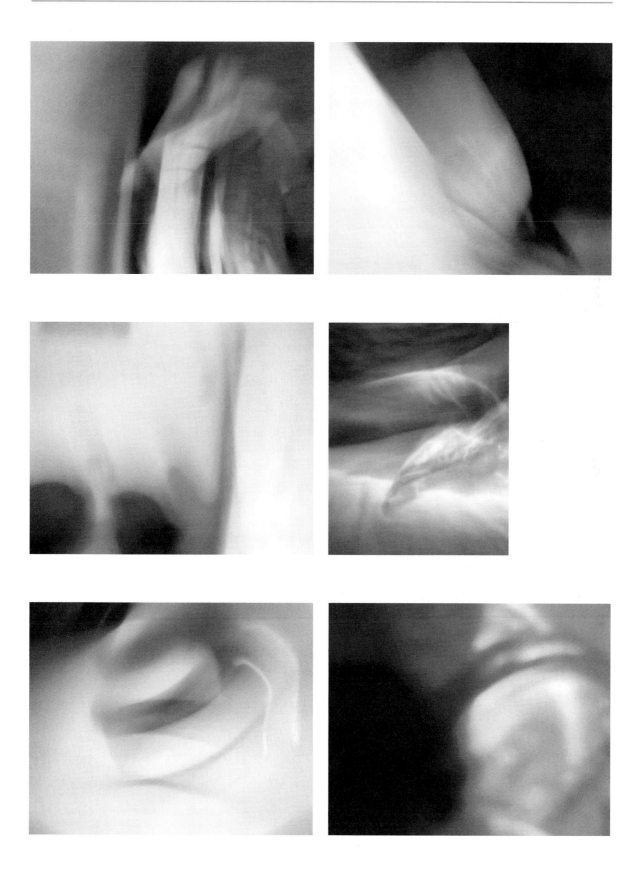

You will be judged on every choice you make

You should be prepared to support and explain the decisions you make. If you have your name stamped on the outside of your portfolio in red and you send a follow up letter to someone who has recently viewed it and your name appears in green, there should be a reason.

You will rarely be asked why you made the decisions that you made. However you will be judged on your level of creativity and consistency. With that being said, I do know an art director who used a different color for his business cards, letterhead, envelopes, and so forth and all very effectively. They were all very striking, rich, bright colors. They were all designed very thoughtfully into a system. For example, yellow was used for the letterhead so it could be typed on while cobalt blue for the business card had reverse type (white letters on the blue card). His work was about color. He distinguished himself as a colorist, and in every sample he managed to apply color in an unexpected and unusual way.

You didn't have to ask him why he used a color because when you saw his presentation it spoke for itself. By the way, his portfolio was cadmium red!

You are in a very competitive environment so you want to make it as easy as possible for the people who receive your communications to remember you.

A consistent vision not only shows someone that you know what you are doing but that you know how to build a brand—your brand. It demonstrates that you know how to market yourself and you understand how to market their product. It also makes it easier for someone to remember you. If Coca-cola changed their label on every can, you would have a very difficult time finding it, wouldn't you?

FIGURE 4.4

The Plexiglas cover portfolio from www.Lost-Luggage.com.

The more familiar someone becomes with your brand, the easier it is to reach them.

Let's say for example that you are a cartoonist and that you have created a series of mailers. Each mailer consists of a hilarious cartoon on a postcard along with all of your contact information. You send out your postcard in a bright red envelope with a funny little illustration on the front of it. So what happens?

The first time someone receives it, it might sit on the desk for a couple of days until he or she gets around to opening the envelope. When he or she finally gets around to opening it, it makes a very positive impression. After a few mailings, not only will he or she recognize it, but he or she will probably look forward to opening it. If it is good enough, it may be one of the first pieces of mail that is opened. The potential client will look forward to them and you have opened a door when you follow up to talk to that person.

Brain share

Although we come equipped with a wonderfully powerful computer in our head and have the ability to remember vast amounts of information, we may not recall all of it all the time. A little nudge is sometimes needed to bring information that we have stored deep in our brains to the forefront of our memory. The more familiar we are with the information, the more likely we are to recall it. The more times we associate a positive experience with whatever it is that we want to remember, the more space it will occupy in our memory.

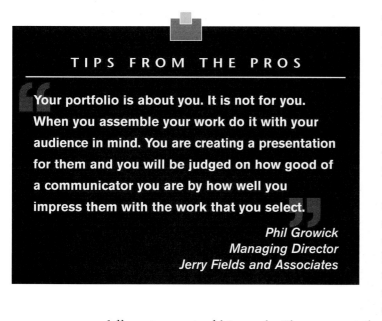

TIPS FROM THE PROS

Your portfolio is about you. It is not for you. When you assemble your work do it with your audience in mind. You are creating a presentation for them and you will be judged on how good of a communicator you are by how well you impress them with the work that you select.

Phil Growick
Managing Director
Jerry Fields and Associates

If all things are equal and you are in competition with three other people for an assignment and you are the one that is foremost in the mind of the potential client when it is time to award the job, your chances will be much better than another who is not. It is a fact that is so incredibly simple, but that many people completely miss it. Don't.

There was a designer who had used a different bold primary or secondary color for his letterhead, envelope, label, and business card but he cleverly brought the colors together for his portfolio. Each section of his portfolio was a different color, and each color introduced a different aspect of his work. The concept that he wanted to get across was that he did several different things and his marketing reinforced it when a client received it.

FIGURE 4.5

Tina Rupp is a tabletop and still life photographer. Attention to the smallest detail is extremely important in her work. She chose to present her work in a square portfolio that was housed in a clamshell portfolio box covered in linen. Her work is printed on paper and bound into the portfolio. She uses her presentation to frame her work and make it the center of attention.

Respect your work and respect the person who is viewing your work

Of course you respect your work. You did it and it is the greatest solution that has ever been created. It is carefully mounted protected by plastic and mounted on a page of black paper. Well, it was like that the last time that you looked. Portfolios get banged and knocked around. Work that is not securely attached, sometimes becomes unhinged and will slide around, displaying your work at an unwanted angle. Someone may take the work out of the sleeve to make a copy (how dare they, but it happens) and maybe place it back upside down or on top of another piece leaving a page blank. Make sure that you are the last person to review your portfolio before it is sent out for viewing. In haste, you may want to rush your book from one company to another, but don't. ALWAYS make sure that you approve your portfolio before it goes out on a showing. A viewer will look through your book once. If there is a problem, they won't ask you to fix it and resubmit it. They will simply move on to the next portfolio.

Some portfolios using plastic sleeves contain black construction paper to mount work. Often this fragile construction paper becomes damaged when the work is changed with other work. The black paper will show tear marks that will detract from the overall presentation. There are some people who prefer not to mount their work with tape because they do not want to damage the paper. Their portfolios often present work that is crooked or has slipped into a corner of a page. Others will mount the work using double-sided tape (the right way to mount it) and when they later change the sample, the page shows signs of damage from the tape removal. Guess what? People will notice. The mounting paper is the least expensive part of a presentation. Do not let a few tears spoil your presentation.

When you have gone to the trouble to carefully measure the position of your work and mounted your work to the page, make sure that you erase the marks you made on the page if they show. Again, people notice.

If your portfolio has dog-eared or torn pages or the portfolio has crushed corners, it makes a statement about your and you work.

However, I remember a portfolio that stood out for being totally decrepit. This was the worst portfolio case I had ever seen. It was torn; pieces of leather were hanging off of it. The handle was wrapped with several different pieces of tape in different colors. It looked like it had traveled the world's worst baggage carrousels. In fact, the outside was covered with travel stickers for different airlines and destinations.

The surprise came when the portfolio was opened to reveal work presented beautifully, tastefully, and perfectly. Even the inside of the portfolio was exquisite. Everything inside looked brand new. The portfolio belonged to an art director who worked exclusively on airline accounts. It made a statement about an art director who had a world of experience and knew how to produce some of the best work in the world. His presentation made perfect sense and delighted the viewer with this creative juxtaposition.

Pay attention to the details—the good ones and the bad. Tape tears and pencil marks may seem like small things, and that is because they are small things. So don't let them become big things and fix them before you show your portfolio.

What tools do you need to assemble your portfolio?

You may not need all of these but here are some basic tools that will make assembling a portfolio easier.

1. An X-acto knife with a few no. 11 blades
2. A pair of scissors
3. A tee square
4. A set square
5. Some double-sided adhesive tape
6. Hinged mounting tape
7. A sharp pencil
8. A ruler
9. An eraser
10. A computer
11. A printer
12. Some great ideas
13. Some patience

FIGURE 4.6

Some of the things you will need to prepare your portfolio.

Computers have changed the way that work is presented. Sometimes the work is printed on the page. Other times, it is printed and mounted onto a page. There are dozens of portfolio types to choose from. There are, however, some things that apply to all portfolios. The suggestions listed here are ones that apply to most situations.

1. Be neat.

2. Make it easy for the viewer.

3. Make it yours. (Let the viewer feel your vision.)

4. Your name, address, and telephone number should be in a prominent location.

If you are using a clamshell presentation and your samples are different sizes, mount all the work on the same size boards. Doing so will make your work easier to handle and make the presentation appear more organized. If you have a specific order for the presentation, you might want to incorporate page numbers into the design of the page. This way it is more likely to remain in the order that you feel delivers the biggest impact.

Typically samples are mounted on black, gray, or white board. There is no reason why they have to be. If you have a reason to mount your presentation on colored boards and believe that is the best way to frame you work, then do so.

The rules for creating a breakthrough portfolio are that there are no rules. Most portfolios show the work presented squarely on the page but that doesn't always have to be the case. One portfolio had a campaign of advertisements mounted so that the ads were on an angle. It stopped the viewer and made him or her realize that all of the ads had photographs that displayed horizon lines that ran parallel to the top and bottom of the portfolio when the ads were angled. Of course, when these ads ran in a magazine the horizon line in the photograph appeared slanted on an angle but in the portfolio showing them in the way they appeared was the strongest way of presenting the concept.

Sometimes an image might fill the page, whereas at other times it may appear smaller in the center of the page. You might want to have one image on one page, several images on a page, or maybe even only part of the image on the page.

The literary world when assessing the merits of a good novel suggests that it should be a *good page turner*. It means that the page being read should grab someone's attention and excites the reader enough to want to turn to the next page.

Your first page of the presentation should be dynamite because that will send the viewer to the next page. It is not his or her responsibility to view the entire book. If it doesn't hold his or her attention, he or she will probably not go past the first few pages.

> Your portfolio must be a good page-turner. You are telling a story, your story. Are you someone who uses humor in your work?
>
> Is your work about how you design elements in a space?
>
> Can color be used to create a thread of continuity?

Is it the idea or the execution of the idea that is more important to communicate?

Should you place light themes next to dark themes or should you move from dark to light?

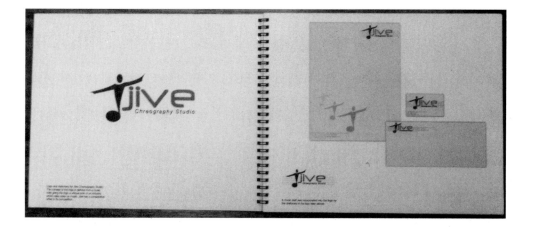

FIGURE 4.7

James Hudson shows here that a good portfolio does not have to be elaborate. With a great design sense and pacing James created a portfolio that was assembled using a wire-bound binding. He made his portfolio more engaging by including a description of the project in a block of copy on every page.

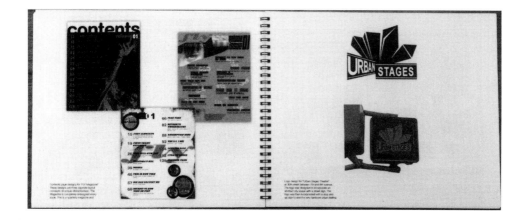

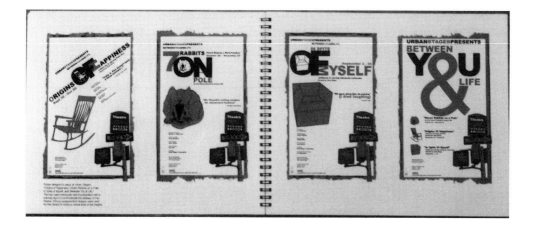

Have you distinguished your voice throughout the portfolio?

Some things you can control and some things you may not be able to. For example some of your sample may be stronger than other ones in your portfolio. Control the things that you can and you may be able to influence the things that you cannot.

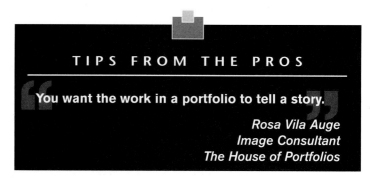

TIPS FROM THE PROS

"You want the work in a portfolio to tell a story."

Rosa Vila Auge
Image Consultant
The House of Portfolios

Mounting work

Whenever you are mounting your work on to a surface whether it is a mat board or sheet of paper make sure that you are working on a large, clean surface. The worst thing you can do is to put a sample of your work on a dirty surface and find a grease stain slowly appearing through a mounted surface. It is also a good idea to keep your coffee or soda on a surface away from where you are working.

I mention these because, although they do not seem like big problems, when you are rushing to put together a portfolio at the last minute they become bigger when you have to start all over again.

Have everything you need so you are not running around trying to find which drawer you put your scissors in. When you have a clean space and your tools at hand, you are ready to begin.

Start by laying out all of the work on the mounting pages to get an idea of the overall *feeling* of the presentation. Sometimes you might start and realize that some of the ideas that you originally had don't fit well with in the overall presentation. For example you might want to place one piece on each page but as you look over the presentation some smaller pieces of work may look better by putting a couple of them next to each other on the same page. These decisions may influence the decision of how and where to center the work on each page. It is better to have this thought out beforehand rather than half way through assembling the work. Think twice, act once.

Next, when you have decided where you will place the work use your ruler, tee square, and set square. Double check that the work appears square on the page, and the borders are consistent throughout the book.

When mounting the work, hinging tape works the best. It is a low-adhesive tape that is gentle on the work. It allows you to carefully remove the work without damage. Some people prefer double-sided tape because it is slightly more permanent but it can damage the mounting material and the work when it is removed.

Work can also be dry mounted onto the mounting surface. Dry mounting requires a dry mounting press. This is permanent. Once the work is dry mounted, it stays attached to the surface it has been attached to. There are times when work is dry mounted to a heavier material. For example when a work is fragile it may be dry mounted to a heavier paper that in turn will be hinge mounted to another surface.

Laminating vs. not laminating

The two general ways to present work are to place it on pages in a portfolio or mount it on mat board in a portfolio box.

Work mounted on mat board in a portfolio box should be mounted on the same size board and should fit snuggly in the box. There are a couple of ways to prepare this work for presentation: You can simply mount the work on mat board and place it in the box as is or you can laminate the work and mounting board. This method can also have a felt pad attached to the back of the laminated board to prevent the back from scratching the top of the board that it sits on.

The laminated board has one advantage: It can be used as a place at your family Sunday dinner and no harm will come to the work. The surface protects the work, although it will pick up scratches over time, and it can easily be cleaned with a soft cloth and a little warm, soapy water. As disadvantages, the laminated board picks up glare from over head light sources when it is presented and once the work is mounted, the mounting is permanent. If you want to remove it to change the size of the presentation or anything else, forget about it. But it is a sturdy long-lasting presentation.

Work mounted without lamination is more susceptible to damage but it is tactile and perhaps more user-friendly. For designers who incorporate final texture of the paper they use in their overall presentation, this form may be a better solution. The work can be easily transferred to another presentation but it is unprotected and being exposed to the elements the work may be more prone to damage.

You will, of course, make the final choice. The choice should depend on what is the solution that will best represent your work. It isn't good enough that your portfolio can be just as good as you can make it, it has to be better than your toughest competition. And guess what, they finished reading this book 6 weeks ago. Here are a few simple things to keep in mind when preparing your work:

1. Establish a rhythm for the placement of your work. If all your work is placed in the center of the page, unless there is a very good reason, do not suddenly place a work off center. It will look like a mistake. Develop a placement system and stick to it. This doesn't mean you have to limit a piece of work to one page, but if your mission is to tell a story with the work, let that story run through the whole portfolio.

2. If you are showing work of the same size on different pages, you want it placed in same page placement. If your presentation displays work *approximately* in the same place on the page, it will tell the viewer that you don't pay attention to detail.

3. If the work is off center or crooked, it will also send out the wrong message. I have had someone apologize when they presented work that was crooked in their portfolio by saying that it must have slipped out of place when they carried it over. Respect your viewer. Make sure that your work is attached well when you are putting your portfolio together and always double check it *before* you show it. It only takes a few minutes to open the portfolio and look through it before you go in for your presentation.

4. If the work, or the page, or the mounting board is worn, ripped, torn, bent, or otherwise damaged, replace it.

5. You are being hired for your work. The viewer should feel that this is one of the, if not the most, important things in your life. Do not stop until it is perfect and be very proud of it.

People who are looking at portfolios view hundreds and hundreds of them. They will spend time with the great ones but not the bad ones.

Rules for computers that you will not find in the user's manual

The computer is an important tool in the preparation of your portfolio but there are a few things that you will want to keep in mind.

1. The closer you are to a deadline, the more problems you will have with your computer.

2. You printer will run out of ink exactly 10 minutes after the store closes.

3. There is a thing that happens when you are ready to open the disc containing samples of your work that you brought home from the office. It usually occurs when you are expecting to print out all the work the night before you have an interview first thing in the morning. When you open the files you get a message telling you that none of the fonts from your office are compatible with the ones on your home computer.

4. The later in the night the bigger the problem.

5. And the problem that was there last night somehow disappeared when you returned from work the next evening.

I will reveal a secret that only Bill Gates and Steven Jobs knew up to now. The secret is as follows: When dealing with computers and printers, do not leave it to the last minute and always have a backup plan.

Computers are great and have revolutionized the way portfolios are put together. They have made it easier *and,* at the same time, harder. Expectations are higher. You cannot make mistakes or show work that is flawed. The excuse that "my concept was better but someone else changed it" or "the client made me do it" does not work any more. If there is a problem with the work you want to show, grab the files and fix it. But understand that computers are only computers. When all is going well they are like a great assistant but when things are not going well, they are merely machines. Do not expect they will understand your problem and roll up their sleeves when you most need it. Give yourself the time to solve any problem that may arise.

The minibook | Computers have raised the bar in terms of creative execution and more is expected of you. They have also spawned a new phenomenon called the mini portfolio.

The miniportfolio is a companion piece that is used as a leave behind or occasionally as an introduction piece. I recommend that you use the miniportfolio sparingly as an introduction. A miniportfolio usually does not present the original work as well as the actual work. This can be a problem if someone is attempting to read copy or see details that are too small. However, it sometimes can be a good way to keep your name in front of a potential client.

A miniportfolio shouldn't be used as the first introduction to your work. If you want to grab someone's attention develop a promotion piece that will entice the person to call you in for an interview or at least call in your portfolio. A minibook lacks the impact of a full-size portfolio and when placed next to one may make a weaker showing.

Only use a miniportfolio as a leave-behind after the portfolio has been viewed. It should be a reminder, not the main presentation. However, I have seen superb minibooks; yet, they weren't just books with samples in them but concepts that included samples.

FIGURE 4.8

Here is a minibook that works. Created by photographer Marc Hauser this 2¼ × 4¼-inch book contains 70 pages of photographs. Marc is a portrait photographer and every page of the book contains one portrait. It give a delightful glimpse into Marc's world.

The leave-behind CD/DVD

More people are using the CD/DVD formats but these can have some pitfalls. A DVD is useful if you have large files and are presenting motion or animated work.

CDs and DVDs often will cause computers to "crash"; thus people generally resist viewing them until the last possible moment. They also take time to launch and navigate. If you have a person's attention and interest, they will probably spend the time to explore it. If someone is looking through a stack of names, they'll probably first look through work that is presented in the easiest format to view.

To summarize, CDs and DVDs can be slow to look at; they are difficult to "flip" through. People do not have a lot of time to spend on exploring a CD/DVD. If someone is very interested in your work, he or she may want to go deeper into it but the first time, but the first "view" is generally only for a quick survey.

CD/DVDs also do not store well. If you have it in a round case, it will roll out of the file folder where it is being stored. Most commonly these discs will go in a stack with others and eventually disappear. I once had the experience of attempting to find a designer for a job. They had sent me a CD with some terrific work. I had thought that I had placed it in a hanging-type file folder in my file cabinet. I have a very organized system but it wasn't there and neither was it in any of the adjacent file folders. Try as I could, I just couldn't find it. To make matters worse I couldn't remember the spelling of her name. Regretfully I awarded the assignment to someone else. A few months ago, my assistant was going through my files and happened to accidentally knock a few CDs out of their files onto the bottom of the filing cabinet. He had to pull out several folders to get at it and, yes, there it was on the bottom of the cabinet along with a few others that went on to the world of the forgotten.

You need to be very selective about what you want to put on a CD/DVD, not all work presents itself well. For example, a printed piece with fine type may not show well. Remember that you will not have control over the browser setting of the viewer. So make sure that you view your presentation on different settings to make sure you are delivering the best presentation that you can deliver.

There are a few things to keep in mind when developing a CD/DVD promotional piece. First, make sure it is labeled with your name and contact information. Many people will put the information on the case, but leave the CD/DVD unlabeled. The moment it comes out of the case and is sitting on a desk with several other unlabeled ones, it will be lost. Spend some time and design and print a professional-looking label. I continually see CD/DVDs that come out of a nicely designed case only to reveal a name scrawled with a magic marker pen.

The biggest problem is that the CD/DVD format is like a treasure box. You cannot tell what is inside until you are inside. So how can you give your presentation the attention that it deserves? A better way to present the CD/DVD presentation is to develop an 8.5′ × 11-inch promotional sheet that your CD/DVD will be attached to. The page should have your name and contact information clearly represented as well as a description and screen shots of the work that is inside. This can be done with an index with pictures or simple text with a montage of images on the page. The idea is to entice your audience to want to see more. It is a promotional piece and should look like one.

The CD/DVD and holder should also be designed well to carry your name and contact information. The user interface should also be designed with an index that makes it easy for the viewer to find what they are looking for.

Why mount it on an 8.5′ × 11-inch paper? If someone likes your work, the piece will go into their files. This presentation will fit into their system easily and be easy for them to retrieve. If the CD/DVD is loose, it will eventually get lost or even drop to the bottom of their filing cabinet. I usually mount the CD/DVD on heavier card stock so it isn't flimsy when handled. Here is another tip. If you place an index tap with your name on it will even be easier to find when it is in the file folder. Be creative with it as well, an index tap with a face looking over the top or what ever will catch someone's attention every time they open the and put a smile on their face.

Other presentation scenarios

There are a number of opportunities for creating unique presentations.

Art galleries

Some art galleries request 35-mm color slides of an artist's work. The slides should be labeled with the dimension and title of the work, the artist's name, a contact number, and an indication to show the viewer the correct way to view the work.

If the scale of the work is important, it is useful to show an installation view. For example in the case of large works, having a picture of the work next to a person may help the viewer understand the context of the piece better.

The work should be numbered and housed in a slide-sheet holder. An accompanying sheet should list the work with titles, dimensions, dates, and materials used in the construction of the work.

Some galleries also accept digital files, so refer to the section on CD/DVD promotional material. The bottom line is that the material must be clearly labeled and easy to access.

Photographers sending mounted transparencies

Photographers once preferred to send their work to advertising agencies as mounted transparencies. Transparencies or chromes when viewed properly over a light box present rich color and show photographers' work well. Photographers have mostly stopped this practice because advertising agencies and design firms prefer to view the work printed, on CD/DVD, or through the photographer's Web site to get a first impression. However, the majority of art buyers still like to receive an actual physical portfolio to judge the work.

Creating pages for a portfolio

There are several ways to display work if you should decide to present your work in a format that uses pages.

The vinyl sleeve

The vinyl sleeve comes in several sizes and can be made to your own specifications. Each page has two parts. First there is an outer vinyl holder that is used to protect the work and hold it in the portfolio. An inner sleeve, usually made of black mat paper, is used to mount the work and it slides into the sleeve.

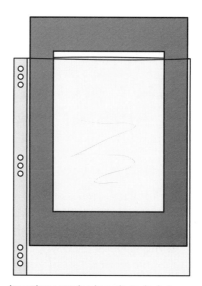

FIGURE 4.9

The samples are mounted on paper and then slid into a vinyl sleeve.

Inserting samples in a clear vinyl sleeve.

One of the simplest ways to hold your work, the vinyl sleeve holds work that is carefully mounted onto a surface like black craft paper and slipped into the sleeve. Your samples can be switched out easily and quickly. It is an easy clean solution.

One problem with the vinyl sleeve is that the vinyl tends to be highly reflective, which can cause a distraction if it reflects the overhead lights or sunlight across your work samples making them difficult to see.

As vinyl ages it can discolor, show scratches, and is susceptible to tearing.

The printed page

Printing your samples on a page and binding the page in a portfolio is another option to consider. Some people have even had their pages printed and bound into a book with a hard cover. This is a very professional solution and if the pages are creatively designed this solution can produce an exceptional presentation.

The printed folio

The printed folio is a very elegant solution; however, once finished, it is impossible to change pages. It usually requires hiring a professional binder to attach the pages and the cover.

Pages are printed using both sides of the paper and several sheets are bound together into a folio. Several folios are then attached and bound into a cover. The finished result is a bound book much like you would buy at the store. The difference is that it is a one-of-a-kind masterpiece.

This solution is best for a person who has collected a body of work and is using this presentation as a record of the work. For example, if a design studio wanted to show a selection of its work that represented a period in its history, this would be a good solution. Another example is a photographer who wants to present a selection of 100 photographs of celebrities or company presidents: This would make a strong presentation.

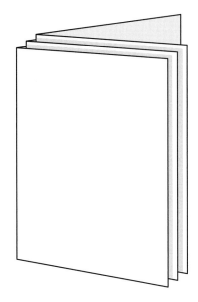

FIGURE 4.10

Folded and printed pages are grouped together.

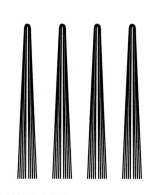

FIGURE 4.11

The folded pages are stitched together.

FIGURE 4.12

The folios are collected and bound together.

FIGURE 4.13

The folios are bound to a cover.

Making a single page

It is most common to present work samples on single sheets, but even when using the single sheet there are many choices to consider. The computer has made it relatively easy to create great presentations on a printed page. The wide selection of paper stocks add to the choices that everyone has today.

FIGURE 4.14

Voila. The French fold is made by folding a single sheet in half. The side opposite the fold is bound into the portfolio.

The French fold

The French fold is not something you do when you make a bed in France—it refers to the way a page is folded. A solution not often seen, it can add a touch of sophistication to a presentation. It can also be helpful to hide problems that are caused by many of today's printers. Some printers can leave offset from a previous page or a dark smudge on the back of a printed sheet. Even though it only appears on the back of a sheet, it can still spoil a presentation.

Many of today's printing papers have been coated only on one side. If you wanted your presentation to be printed on the front and back of a page, you would have to mount another page to the backside of the page or use a French fold. The French fold is simply achieved by folding a piece of paper in half so that the front and back of a page are on the same side of the paper.

Hinging a page

If you are using the French fold or the single sheet of paper with a sample of your work printed on it, you might want to consider hinging the paper to make the pages open easily and lie flat.

To hinge a page you need a page, a hinge, and some hinging tape. The hinge can be made from the same paper that you use for your page. It should be wide enough to fit within the binding. Whatever fasteners you are using it is advisable to punch the holes on the hinges to accept the fasteners before you attach them to the pages. The hinges should be made by folding a narrow strip of paper approximately 1 to 1.5 inches and punching holes where they will be fastened to the portfolio.

The hinge is then laid next to the page with approximately a 1/32 inch of space between the hinge and page. Apply 1-inch hinging tape the full length of

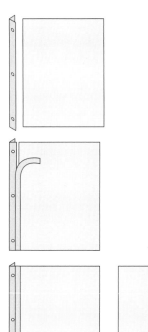

FIGURE 4.15

How to make a hinged page. **1**, Score and fold a 3-inch–wide piece of paper that is the exact height of the page. Carefully select position for holes for binding and make them with a paper punch. **2**, Using hinging tape fasten one side of the paper to the hinge. **3**, Fasten the backside of the paper to the hinge.

the height of the paper and hinge. Turn the page over and apply the hinge tape to the back side of hinge and paper. You have just created a beautifully hinged page ready to display in your new portfolio. Wow! Now that looks professional and it will lie flat when it is being viewed.

And now the outside

Portfolios have an inside and an outside. Whatever you do you should make sure it reflects who you are. In Chapter 2, I laid out a system for defining your vision or brand. The system helped you develop a key set of words to describe you and your work, but there is more to the system. This system also can be used to help guide the colors you choose and the typography you use for your personal identity.

TIPS FROM THE PROS

"You shouldn't ever have to apologize for any thing in your book. If there is a problem fix it. If there is something you can't fix, don't put it in your book. It is much better to have fewer samples and a strong book than a portfolio with a lot of work containing pieces that are not strong. Always leave the viewer excited about your work and wanting to see more. An inconsistent portfolio will leave the viewer with the feeling that he or she has seen too much. It will also tell the viewer that you cannot tell good work from bad. Would you give a job or assignment to someone if you didn't trust the quality of the work that will be delivered?"

Jeannette Trout
Human Resources, AvenueA/Razorfish

Color and typography have properties that communicate different values. It is something that every creative person knows or should know. Earlier in this text you built an individual vision profile that was constructed using words. Here is a way to translate those words into a visual system. Color, typography, and words all have properties and communicate different senses. For example, if I said the word *wedding* and asked you to select a color and typeface example that suggested wedding, you would probably choose the color white and a type face with a serif or in a script type.

The following system is meant to be a guide for you. It helps you to align your message in a very concrete way. Of course, as I have said throughout this book, THIS IS A GUIDE. If there is a reason not to follow these suggestions, don't. But make sure whatever you do has a reason behind it.

Color and typography can be defined in terms of being warm and cool, soft and hard. In Chapter 2 you used words to define your vision now you can take these words and apply them to the following graph.

SOFT

WARM　　　　　　　　　COOL

HARD

Now start to add the words to this graph. For example clean, crisp, and contemporary would fall in the right side of the graph. The colors would be on the cooler side and a typography choice would fall into the san serif category.

SOFT

Pastel rose　　　　　　Pastel blue

WARM　　　　　　　　　COOL
　　　　　　　　　　　　Ice blue
Cadmium red　　　　　Black

HARD

If you were to develop a logo for yourself, it would follow the same system. Let's say you are an architectural photographer who specializes in very graphic modern buildings. You would probably have a cooler color scheme and san serif type. Your logo would be clean. The stationary that you would select would be crisp, clean, and bright white. An architectural photographer specializing in dwellings like old farms, cottages, and woodsy-type places would choose a much warmer combination of type and color. The photographer's logo would have more traditional features like serif type.

SOFT
Script
WARM　　　　　　　　　COOL
Palatino　　Times Roman　　Antique Olive
　　　　　　Helvetica
HARD

If you are a young hot art director then everything from your business card to portfolio should sizzle. If you are a leading edge fashion photographer then you must be prepared to make a statement that will have every fashion editor talking not only when they open your portfolio but when they open a letter from you as well. The paper that you choose for your letterhead is as important as the sample you choose for your portfolio.

You can have your name or logo embossed, stamped, printed, etched, or attached on a brass or plastic plate onto your portfolio. You can take the type treatment that you have selected to represent yourself and go to a local sign company and have them cut vinyl letters for you that you can attach to the outside of your book. You can find dimensional letters from a local hobby store and attach them to your portfolio. They can be attached directly or placed under a vinyl sheet to give an impression of embossed letters. You can place a stencil and spray paint your name. The options are as unlimited as your imagination.

I had a visit from a designer who wanted to open a design business. He had a free office space (his parents' converted garage) and lots of ideas. A call came in one morning from him and he was in a panic, asking to see me right away.

When he arrived, he pulled out a pile of estimates from his knapsack and dropped them on my table. "I'll never have a business!" he exclaimed. "Look at these numbers! I can't afford this."

The estimates covered the cost of business cards, letterhead, envelopes, estimates forms, signage, and so forth. The total was well over $15,000.

He had created a wonderful but complicated design and it was obvious that the design contributed to the overall expense, but that was not all. To ensure that it would be cost efficient to print everything, he had very large quantities of everything.

First we analyzed his needs to get started in business. Did he really need 10,000 letterheads to start his business? The answer was no. The design was great, but it required three colors to print the job. Although he was very attached to the design, as we discussed it he realized that as a designer, part of his assignment for others was finding solutions that work.

His color printer would provide him with a continuous supply of letterheads and business material. A simplified design would make it easier to create signage and other materials.

A few days later, he arrived back at my studio. The first thing I noticed was a new red logo on the side of his car. It was simple and very effective a circle with a slice cut out of it that reflected the use of negative and positive space and conveyed the initials of his company. He had a simple and elegant design that was simple enough that he was able to cut his own vinyl logo and apply it to his car. He produced a portfolio with the same mark on it and inside produced his corporate material he had done all this on his own—created, printed or constructed by hand. He had put together a complete corporate identity and all it took was a lot of creativity and a weekend.

ASSIGNMENT

Dare to BE Great

1. Create three logos or signatures that represent and support your personal brand. What colors would you use? What typeface best conveys your image? How would you transfer your logo to your portfolio?

   Return to the vision statement and review your work. How does your logo support the claims that you make. Now select the one that best supports your vision. This will be your logo.

2. Explore a few ways to present your work. Mount your work on matt board, slip in into vinyl pages, and print it onto a page. How do they feel when you look through the work? Which method best presents your work? Which method tells the story that you want to convey? By trying different methods, you will get a sense of how others might react to your presentation. Practice a presentation using these different presentation pieces. Which feels more comfortable?

Does your logo or signature appear on every page? Is there a title page that introduces your vision? Change the order of your work. How does a different order change the impact of the portfolio?

Try a practice presentation on a friend. What you want to do is watch how someone reacts to the presentation. This is a good exercise to learn when you are presenting your work to others. Their reaction will guide you through the presentation, so watch them carefully.

Often times when you are presenting you are excited or nervous and want to get through the presentation as quickly as possible, but don't. Watch your audience, they will give you the clues you need for a successful presentation. If while presenting your work you turn the page and notice that the viewer shows a little more interest, spend a little more time talking about the sample or ask them what they find interesting about the work.

The more information you gain from the viewer the easier your job will become because you will understand what they are looking for. This will help you better understand how to speak to them.

Marketing

The follow through

Networking and marketing

Did you know that the best place to find empty Altoids cans is at hair salons?

Now why would that have anything to do with promoting your work?

If you want your work to be seen as being creative, you must present it in a creative way. As one photographer discovered, the smaller your promotional budget, the more creative you will need to be.

A photographer was just finishing off the last Altoids breath mint and admiring the can it came in when an idea struck him: Why not use the empty can as a portfolio for his work? After a few experiments, he found a way to remove all the paint from the can and then created a stamp that would emboss his name and Web address on the top of the lid. Perfect, except for one problem. Someone would have to eat a lot of Altoids to get enough empty cans to develop an effective marketing program. So he had a great idea, but realized it would take a couple of years to save up enough Altoids cans even if he got help from all of his friends.

Saved by the girlfriend

It started with his girlfriend. He asked her if she would mind eating a few more Altoids—actually boxes of Altoids—than she normally did every day. He explained it was not because she needed fresh breath but simply because he needed the boxes.

The next day a solution presented itself when his girlfriend arrived with blue hair and fuchsia tips dyed only moments ago at her favorite hair salon. As her boyfriend was stripping the paint off of a shipment of several Altoids boxes from friends, his girlfriend mentioned that the hairdressers had a box of Altoids at every station. Further investigation revealed that among service businesses where vendors work in very close proximity with their clients, vendors try to make the clients' experience as pleasant as possible by popping breath mints before meeting each new client. Telephoning local hair establishments revealed

FIGURE 5.1

Chie Ushio's promotional pieces are imaginative and fun and the type of thing that will find its way pinned up over someone's desk as a reminder.

an abundance of empty Altoids boxes that were about to be discarded. By asking several salons to save their empty boxes, the photographer found an unending supply of tools for his marketing. Thus, a promotion was born–inexpensive, unique, and effective. After a while the demand for this unique marketing idea created such a level of demand for the photographer's services that the photographer finally had to find the manufacturer of the boxes and buy them directly.

The conclusion: Good and effective ideas do not have to cost a lot, but they do have to be good enough to set you apart from your competition.

Great you've got their attention. Now what?

Absolutely fabulous meeting, they loved the book, the interview went well, everyone shared the same interests but 3 weeks have passed, and you have not received a return call. Well they do not appear to be interested so it is time to move on to the next prospect, right?

Wrong.

Stop. Hold everything. Maybe they are sitting in their offices saying,

It was an absolutely fabulous meeting. We loved the book. Lunch went well. We shared the same interests. But it has been 3 weeks and he hasn't called. Guess he's not interested. Better move on to the next candidate.

When someone is looking for a candidate for a job or assignment, they are looking for a guarantee that the person has the skills to do it; will do the work on time, within budget, and without problems; and *is interested in doing the work.* That seems simple, but it doesn't always happen, and people who have experience hiring people have had the experience of hiring people who do not work out.

Your actions can help the process or hinder it. They will expect that you are a responsible, committed person. If you have the opportunity to meet with them and get them excited about the possibility of working with you and do not follow up, your inaction will reflect on your commitment and not in a good way. The follow-up also helps them know you better because it is the start of building a relationship. The decision to hire is based on the comfort level that (a) the person can the person do the work and (b) they want to be around the person.

It also is your opportunity to see if these are the people who you want to work with. You should take any opportunity to meet, talk, and e-mail people who you are considering working with. The more you know about them—and the more they know about you—the better are your chances for success.

People who hire look for certain things:

They hire people who they have worked with before and who they have confidence through direct knowledge that the person can do the job.

They hire people who are referred by people they have confidence in because they have referred competent people before.

They hire people who have a reputation for delivering.

They hire people who they know because they know these people well enough to believe that the person can deliver.

Then they hire people who they do not know but who have a level of work that they are looking for and references of people in responsible positions who can recommend them.

What does this list tell you and where do you fall into it? It tells you that if you drop out of the sky with an incredible portfolio, it may be a difficult road unless you have an excellent story to go along with it. However, if you enter the scene with a breakthrough portfolio along with a reference to open a door, your chances for success are greatly improved.

Marketing yourself is no different from marketing a product. First, you need a product, which in this case is yourself. Second, you need to define your market. Your market is the people who will be interested in the product. You must find a way to communicate the value of the product to the group in a way that they will understand how that value will benefit them. This includes communicating with them in a way that demonstrates your uniqueness. You will need to build a core group that will commit to your product and continue to build on that group. Then you will stay in touch with your network to help you find where there is demand for your talent.

Have you ever met those people who seem to have it so easy? They get what they want. They always seem to know a lot of people who they can call to get what they want or are able to connect to someone who gets them what they want.

People in the communications business surprise me because when it comes to promoting themselves, they seem to forget everything they know about advertising. After all, *you* should be your most important product. If direct mail works to make consumers aware of a product, it also will make people aware of you. This is also true for telemarketing, billboards, posters, and so forth. If you write radio commercials, make a great radio commercial to promote yourself and send it along with your resume. Not only impress someone with your resume but also demonstrate how good you are by using what you do to communicate it.

And then the follow up

You have spent a lot of time and effort to meet people but meeting them is not enough. You must continue to keep yourself in their sights. Perhaps the job or assignment that you were hoping for didn't materialize, but by keeping connected with the people you have met, you are building a bridge that will contribute to your success.

Being the "it" girl, boy, woman, or man

Did you ever notice that there are some people who always end up in the right spot at the right time? Do you want to know how you find out where that spot is? Here is how you do it.

Get involved. If you are starting out and you want to work for the best company on the planet and there are no positions available, call and get on to their intern program. If they don't have an intern program, ask if you could be the first.

There are two types of interns: one who interns to get the name of a company on his or her resume and the other who wants a job. The latter wants the people around him or her to know that they will do what it takes to work with that company. It is easy to spot both types. The first, working for free or for a small stipend, has a list of reasons why he or she comes in late or must leave early or has another appointment that will mean more time off.

The other has an attitude of "no I don't know how to do that but show me once and I will" accompanied by "is there anything else I can do?"

At the end of the internship, when one of them is offered a position, which one do you think gets it and which one do you think says, "Yeah. What do you expect? He always gets everything."

Being "it" means being involved.

No matter where you are in your career, there are always places where you can go to connect. Many assignment creatives or freelancers often comment that they feel disconnected because they work by themselves. They don't have to be disconnected.

In every city, there are clubs and associations that are there to help people to connect with one another. Art director clubs, illustrator clubs, photography association, business associations, public speaking groups, book clubs, and so forth. In fact, there are hundreds of places where you can go to connect with people to meet potential clients and potential employers. The more you connect with these clubs and organizations, the more you connect to your community. Your community may be the city you live in, the country you live in, or the world itself depending on whom you connect with.

FIGURE 5.2

Photographer Chip Forelli worked with designer Ron Burkhardt to develop a set of beautiful promotional posters for his work that can be framed. I spoke to Chip recently and he mentioned that he was having the best year of his professional life and attributes some of this success to his promotion.

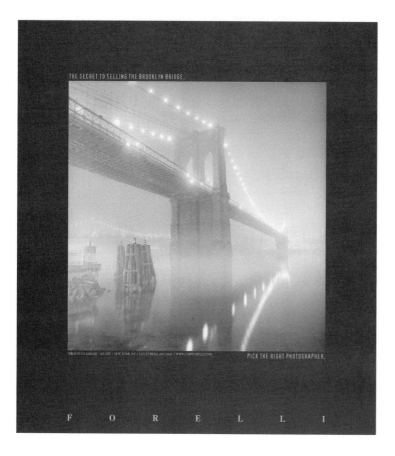

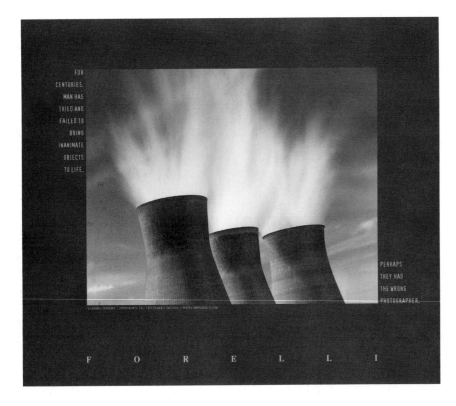

FOR CENTURIES, MAN HAS TRIED AND FAILED TO BRING INANIMATE OBJECTS TO LIFE.

PERHAPS THEY HAD THE WRONG PHOTOGRAPHER.

F   O   R   E   L   L   I

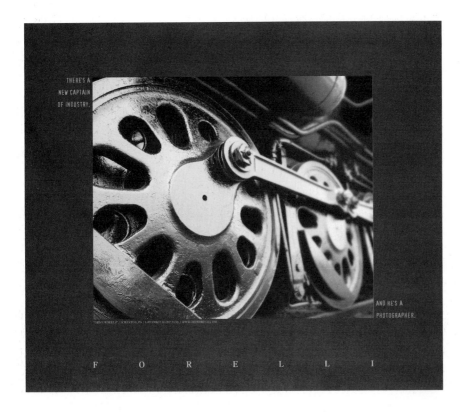

THERE'S A NEW CAPTAIN OF INDUSTRY.

AND HE'S A PHOTOGRAPHER.

F   O   R   E   L   L   I

And now, the secret to being the "it" person

You have to get involved. If you join an art director's club and never attend any events or if you rarely talk to anyone at the events, your experience will not be rewarding. But once you get involved, become chairperson of an event or president of the club, guess what, you have become "it." You have become the person that others seek out. You have placed yourself in a position where others want you in their network. Having you in their network of course puts them in your network and the more networks you are a part of, the more connected you are to what is happening in your industry. And it is easy—most clubs and association welcome with open arms anyone who volunteers for any of their many committees. So find one and join in.

FIGURE 5.3

Zave Smith has worked hard to achieve the level of success he now has. Being a great photographer was not enough—he had to repeatedly gain the attention of his audience through innovative and exciting marketing pieces like the ones here. A clever addition to this set of promotional items was the inclusion of a postcard that reminded the receiver to visit his Web site for his latest work.

There are only five people in your business

As you are meeting people on your job search, you are beginning to build a network. After a while, you will begin to see a pattern emerging. The decision makers start to show up time and time again. Whether they are on the board of directors at local clubs or speaking at events or written about in magazines, the same names will appear over and over again as will the names of their friends in business. These are good people for you to have in your network and good people to stay in touch with.

Remember earlier I mentioned that people like to give work to people who they know? Well this is how you put yourself in a position to be known to them: The people who you meet won't necessarily all have the job you are looking for or be in the position at the moment to give you the job you want, but one day they might. This is an important key to the success of your career.

Countless times opportunities die because they are not followed up. It as simple as that. Maybe you sent one e-mail or left one voice mail, but when nothing came of it, you stopped. I can guarantee that the person who got the assignment or job did not stop.

It is all about making a connection. Making a connection is not about showing up and showing someone your portfolio. It is about making a connection with them. Showing them something in you that persuades them that you are the person for them. Your portfolio is a tool that you can use to help you find the connection.

How to present a portfolio

People are often in such a hurry to show their portfolio that they never really make a connection to the person who is viewing it. They quickly open the portfolio and relinquish all their power to the interviewer. *You never ever want do this.* The moment you do this, you give the interviewer the power to say those dreaded words, "Thanks, but this isn't what we are looking for."

A University of Toledo study concluded that the first 30 seconds makes or breaks communication between two people when they meet for the first time. In other words, the next time you have an interview, the interviewer may be drawing conclusions about you before you even get to the interview. Take a moment and make a connection before you show your work. Set the tone for the meeting—it will help influence the person who you are presenting your work to.

An effective way of presenting a portfolio is to keep it closed until the interview has answered a few questions. It is time to open the portfolio only when you have an idea of what the interviewer is looking for and an insight into his or her personality. This can easily be accomplished by asking a few simple questions. The following represent a few questions that will give you a head start:

What exactly are you looking for?

What are the requirements for this position?

Are there specific skills that you are looking for?

FIGURE 5.4

Brian Ponto creates interactive pieces that are truly engaging. For a promotional piece, he sent out this clever bumper sticker. I have seen it on the walls of several companies that I have visited.

What is the exact scope of the project (or assignment)?

Can you show me the work that was done on the account before?

What do I have to do to convince you I am perfect for this?

Now by asking these questions, you have set some boundaries that can help you guide the interviewer through their book. You can begin by saying, "Great. I think that there are several samples in my book that demonstrate exactly what you are looking for." Then let the interviewer look through your portfolio and let him do the talking. He may well say, "Yes I can see why you say you have the skills for this position." Or, he might say, "And which pieces demonstrate _____?" At which point you have an idea what he was looking for and be in a better position—having had some time to think about it—to answer his question. You are then able to address why you believe you are right for a project although you may not have demonstrated it in your portfolio.

We often think we know what is going on, but we only know what we think is going on and not what is actually happening. There are a hundred reasons that someone does not call you back—including the one that you are not right for this particular job. However,

TIPS FROM THE PROS

VISION

"We tend to think of vision in terms of observing the world, of looking from the inside out. But for artists, vision is what we show to the world, and how we distinguish ourselves in the world. Vision is how we connect to others through the iterative crafting our intensely personal expression. It is through this personal vision we add a human dimension to the world of commerce. The rest is just typography."

Stephen Pite Dean
Design and Digital Media
Katharine Gibbs,
New York City

another reason could be that they thought that someone wanted it more than you seemed to want it. The ideal job or project could be lost simply because you didn't make that one follow-up telephone call.

Staying in touch is one of the most important ways to give your career life and longevity. The hardest thing is getting in the door the first time. After you become known it gets easier and easier for you. The secret is to stay in touch.

What happens if you are chasing a position with several companies and you finally get an offer and accept a position from one of them? No reason to talk to the other companies again, right? Wrong. This is one of the best times to talk to them.

You have increased your value in their eyes because your worth has just been confirmed by a third party. In other words, you were an unknown entity to them and now someone else has made it easy for them because they have given you a chance to prove your value.

One of the most successful creative individuals I know carries two Palm Pilots to hold all of his contact information. He is also one of the most generous people I know when it comes to helping people. He is a successful director in a company and he got his present position because one of his contacts called to ask him if he knew any potential candidates for this position. As the position was being described to him, he said, "You know, that sounds like something I would be interested in doing." He was called because he placed himself in a position where he could offer value to others. He became connected into a network because of what he offered. This put him in a position to know what was going on around him all the time. He is in the game and not on the outside looking in. He is a player.

One of the reasons that you might not get a job or assignment is that you did not show the skills for the particular job that they had at that particular moment. However, the next position they have might be a perfect fit.

There's the short term and then there is the commitment to building a successful career. It takes time.

FIGURE 5.5

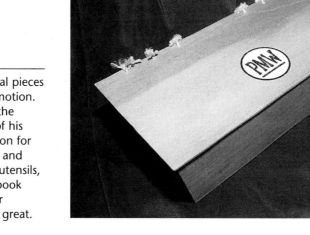

One of the more ambitious promotional pieces is Paul Mathew Woods' barbeque promotion. Paul's appreciation and knowledge of the southern barbeque is so much a part of his personality that it became the inspiration for his idea. A wooden box contains a red and white checkered place mat, barbeque utensils, barbeque recipes, and a promotional book that ties barbeque and design together perfectly. By the way, the recipes were great.

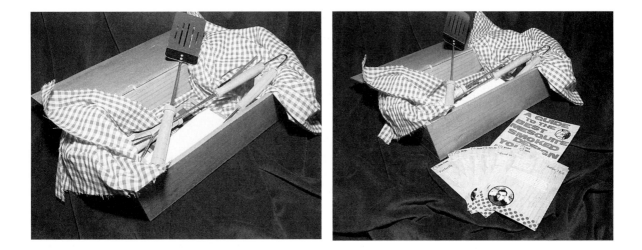

There are only five people in your business

It may seem like a daunting task in the beginning, but the working world is a lot smaller than you think.

There are a finite number of headhunters, creative managers, and employers. Over the years, people may change positions or companies or they may leave a company and form their own company, but once you understand the lay of the land it will become surprisingly simple to fit in.

Keeping connected

Follow up is probably the single most important marketing and networking tool. Most follow-ups are done poorly or not at all. People will spend an enormous amount of time of time and energy perfecting their portfolios and preparing for an interview, only to walk away from the opportunity when they leave the company's office. Maybe a telephone call or two will be placed or a thank you letter will be sent, and if the person does not receive a return call or get another offer she or he will give up. If you want to be successful, never remove yourself from the game.

Do not take it personally. There are several thousand reasons that people do not get back to you. Perhaps they misplaced your contact information or perhaps they are just too busy. It may be that you may not be right for the position.

Keep a contact list and follow up. Keep in touch.

How to keep in touch

In previous sections I suggested getting involved in clubs or associations for art directors photographers, architects, illustrators, directors, or a number of other types. This is a good place to keep in touch and discover what others are doing. Other ways to keep in touch include the following:

Keep your name current by writing articles for trade magazine, attending industry award shows, conventions, joining company softball teams, or other events.

Send a holiday card. Pick a holiday—it doesn't have to be at the end of the year. Make up a holiday such as Happy Art Director's week.

Announce the winning of an award.

Announce a new position or new project.

KEEP IN TOUCH because the next time someone is looking to hire someone or hand out an assignment, they will not dig very deeply into their pile. The person who is top of mind will be the one who gets the call. Be at the top of mind!

You are most valuable when you are working. When you are working you have been validated at least in the eyes of others. You want to contact all of the other people who you saw on your search for work and inform them of your status.

The professional resume

There are hundreds of books offering advice on building a resume, but very few offering guidance on the building of a resume for a creative person.

Even if you are freelancing or working independently, a resume is important. A resume is another tool to extend your brand or your vision. It gives you an opportunity to present a more intimate picture of yourself. It is an opportunity to give an insight.

What is normal?

Normal is a cycle on a washing machine. What you want to achieve is to set yourself apart from your competition in everything that you do. It could be as simple as your name, contact information, vision statement, and list of clients or awards. The more traditional resume is a listing of work history and experience.

It may be necessary to have several resumes and customize them for each presentation. If you were approaching a client whose specialty is fashion accessories, it would be wise to reflect your experience in that industry in the beginning of the resume.

A brief look at different types of resumes

All resumes do not have to be the same.

Listing skills

You can begin a resume by listing your skills. For example all the computer programs that you have expertise with then follow it with work history.

Listing work history

You can begin with a listing of work history and related accomplishments. However, keep it specific to the job you are applying for. Do not list the year that you were a lifeguard in high school unless you specialize in sports photography, which is only when it might that matter.

If you list a skill, make sure you can do it. Speaking Spanish fluently means speaking Spanish fluently. If you have added it to your resume because it will help you get the job but you only have high school—level Spanish, be aware that when you are found out it will put into question everything else on your resume.

Keep it relevant, keep it interesting. Find something that is unique about you and relate it to how that embellishes what you do.

A resume has to be read. Tiny type can look cool but if no one can read it, it is not that cool.

The success triangle

There are some jobs where everything feels right but others where they don't. The following is a strategy that can help you with your decisions.

The success triangle is only a guide, but many professional have found it useful when deciding whether to accept a job. Ideally you should be able to accept projects that include all three

However at the least it should have two.

1. Make money

   This one should be pretty obvious. If you work you want to get paid.

2. Build your book

   Do work that will bring you more work, add a great addition to your portfolio, or improve your skills

3. Meet the right people

   Meet people who can get you to the type of work you want to do or to other people who can get you the work your want.

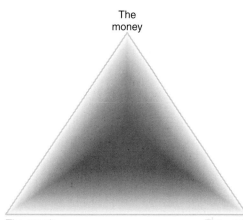

The money

The people   The work

FIGURE 5.6

The success triangle is a tool to that can help you in the decision process when you are considering accepting an assignment.

If you are accepting work only for money, you will end up unsatisfied and doing more work that may not improve your career or get you work that will pay you more.

If you are only doing work that you like or will improve your skills, sooner or later you are not going to be able to afford to continue doing it.

If you are doing work with people who can't give you the type of work you want to do, you will find it very unfulfilling and it will not progress your career.

e-mail

The thank you note

Telephone

Billboard

Carrier pigeons

Marketing yourself

A photographer once delivered carrier pigeons to potential clients. The pigeons had message bottles attached to their legs that messages could be put in and delivered to the photographer via the pigeons. Did he get work? You bet he did. Not only that—it was over 20 years ago and people still talk about it.

I received a well-designed mouse pad with your resume printed on it and a message: This is to keep my resume on your desk rather than in your desk. Did it stay on my desk? Yes it did.

There are hundreds of ways to get people's attention. Only a few appear in this list:

Sandwich boards

Telegram (people still read them)

FedEx (who won't open a FedEx package?)

T-shirt

BUT—and this is a really big but—whatever you do must be done well. It must be done creatively. It must be done with taste. It must be interesting to the receiver.

If you send a FedEx package with a T-shirt in it that says, "I want a job," it will probably end up in someone's waste basket.

You are creating a piece of communication that you want to represent you. If you have to think about this go back and reread Chapter 2. What does your vision sound like? If you send out a CD with music, does the sound design support your vision?

You are a designer of high-end, new-age spas and spa treatments. You wouldn't want to accompany your vision with a musical from Metallica. Everything you do goes together to support your vision be sure what you send out supports your image.

ASSIGNMENT

The assignment is to develop a marketing piece. The first thing to remember is that it is from you and not for you. It should represent you, deliver your vision, and excite someone enough to pick up the telephone or e-mail you.

Review your vision statement and your color and typography guide.

If someone tacked the piece up on the wall, is your contact information visible? If they put it in their file, will it be easy to find? How is this piece packaged or is it its own package?

Develop three different promotional pieces and pass them to friends along with the following survey.

What does this say about me?

What type of work am I offering?

Do you know how to contact me?

Did you find this piece interesting?

Would this make you contact me?

On the scale of 1 to 5 with 1 being the lowest score and 5 being the highest, how would you rate its effectiveness?

Do you have any suggestions to improve it?

CHAPTER 6

The Career Path

The path to a great career

Your portfolio is a single element in a successful career. It should be used to display your talent and to keep people aware of your evolving talent.

It can be used as a strategic tool even when someone might not have an assignment or position for you. You can bring your book or send your Web site to someone to ask him or her for comments about some new work or to get some advice on the flow of work. People will respect and support your determination to keep your book current and effective.

You are in a business that will require more of you than most. It may and should be your passion because those hiring you will certainly expect you to be passionate about what you do. They will also expect you to be knowledgeable not only about your craft but about their business as well.

Expectations are high at every level–from someone entering the market to someone with years of experience. There is a saying that very much holds true, "You are only as good as your last assignment."

A photographer was awarded his first job from an important agency. As he began to develop the project, he realized that he was in a little over his head and the project was turning out to be much more complicated that he thought it would be. He worked harder than he had ever worked doing 20-hour days and had worked 48 hours straight a couple of times. After 3 weeks he had completed the work and brought it over to the people at the agency who were thrilled with the work.

The photographer, relieved and looking for a little sympathy, then began telling them how hard he worked and how many long hours he had put in to complete the work on time. At that point the at director cut him short saying, "Thank you delivered the job that you promised and what we expected but we don't need to know about your journey to get there."

Whatever assignment you are given, it is expected that you would produce a professional piece of work. There probably isn't one successful person in this business who hasn't worked night and day on some project somewhere in their career. That's just how it is.

You will be given latitude, being a creative person, but the latitude will depend on their structure and your performance. If you are able to turn words and images into gold, (translated as profit for your client and awards and profit for your company) you will be given more opportunities to express more of your individual vision.

The more clear the picture you have of the industry you are about to enter, the better are your chances of succeeding in it. If you are carrying any unanswered questions as you move into or through your chosen profession, ask someone. If you don't know anyone personally who can answer the question, there are ways to find the answers. This does not only apply to people entering the market; it also applies to people already working in the market. The more clear the picture you have of where you fit into the puzzle and what you have to do to be where you want to be, the better are your chances of succeeding.

A book illustrator may not know if his or her style will translate to advertising illustration. The illustrator could develop a marketing program and send out promotional pieces to agencies and place ads in publications; however, these cost money and may or may not bring results. The illustrator could also call a few art buyers at ad agencies and ask for a few minutes of their time for their advice. The illustrator could also join an art director's club in the area and network with some of the people. By doing either of these, the illustrator will get a better understanding of how his or her work may fit into the market and is building a network of potential clients. There always is a way to find the information that you need and it usually comes from talking to people. In addition, even if the first few telephone calls do not get you in front of the right person, it will sooner than later get you to where you need to be.

It is the same with a new portfolio. Most people in this business have at one time or another asked others for advice, and most, if approached with respect, will do the same for you. This will not only help you with some positive direction but it can be the first step in building your network. There are dozens of sources to find people, ranging from trade magazines to award publications to trade organization to relatives. And most people will likely give you time. The key is knowing who you are calling.

FIGURE 6.1

Hitomi Watanabe is Puce Graphics. Wananabe's Web site is first and foremost about the work. The site's simple but strong presentation supports the work and the brand. Navigation makes it easy to get to the portfolio and each page adds more excitement in the way the work is presented.

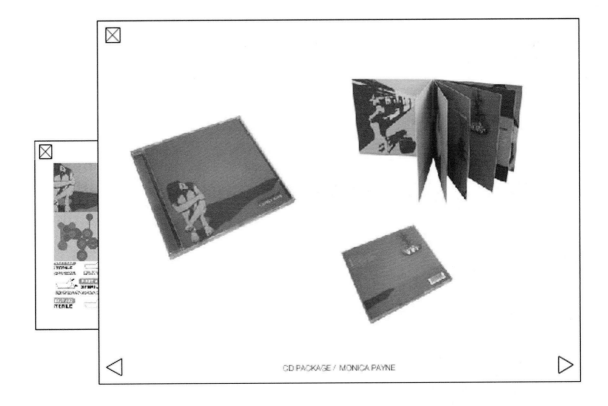

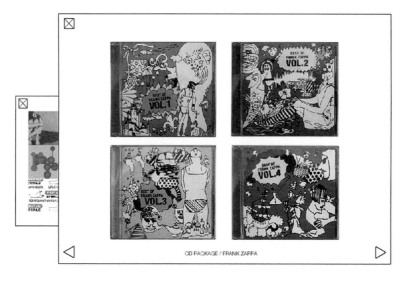

CD PACKAGE / FRANK ZAPPA

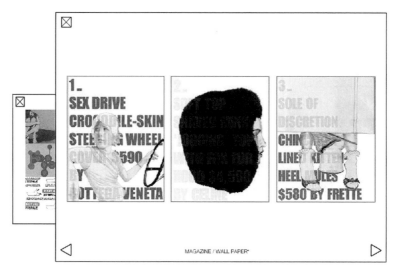

MAGAZINE / WALL PAPER*

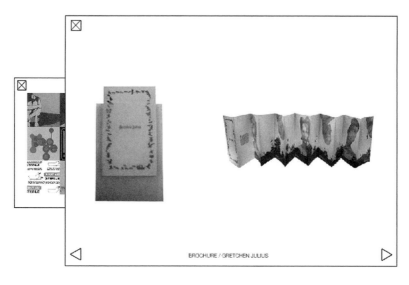

BROCHURE / GRETCHEN JULIUS

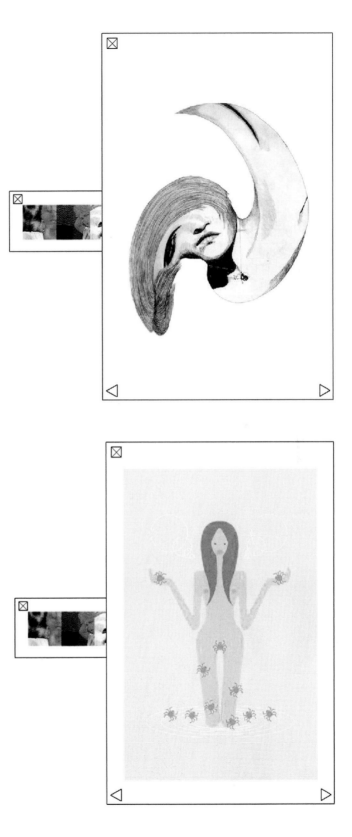

Do your homework first

Approaching a person when you are familiar with their work will give you a connection when talking with them. A person will be interested in talking to you about your work if your work is interesting to them. Choose someone in your field. If you are an environmental designer, do not call the creative director of an advertising agency because he or she probably will not be interested in helping you and will probably not have a lot of useful information. Be selective and do your research.

It may take a few telephone calls—people may be busy or overcommitted—but if you persevere, you will find someone to sit and talk with you. You can always send a letter first telling them that you will follow up by phone. However if you do send a letter follow up. A word of caution: Do not send out a mass mailing because you may get more responses than you bargained for. Send out a few requests at a time, following up on them as you do.

Do NOT send anything to anyone who you will not follow up with.

Many people, I would hazard a guess the majority of people, will not follow this advice. They feel uncomfortable for one reason or another about calling people they do not know. This is a great opportunity for you. While others are making excuses, you will be making connections. This works whether you are new to the marketplace or a seasoned veteran. You would expect that someone who has been in the business for years would understand this and act on it. The veteran is usually more unlikely to do it. Perhaps after being in the business for a number of years, the experienced veteran feels uncomfortable about showing that she or he might not understand a portion of the business. However cultivating ignorance is not a formula for success. Here's a tip: Anyone in business can always use a few more good contacts and a little more good advice.

You might even get a job offer or even a mentor. Many successful people place themselves in positions where they can find great creative talent. It is great talent that is always looking to hire great talent to keep them at the top.

table of contents

type foundry poster
typography in the 20th century book
butterfly stamp and poster
pottery show poster
bioclimatic architecture
urban stages promotional
schelles logo and packaging
moteia packaging and stationary
chocolate bars
tri-tips stationary and advertisements
magazine design
ecotourism book

FIGURE 6.2

Farah Qureshi cleverly designed her logo with an image and a puzzle. When four of her business cards are seen, the design of a complete butterfly is realized. The design fragments add playfulness to her identity program and variety and versatility.

Next step: Yes, there are always next steps

You have met with a person whom you respect and they have given you 15 undivided minutes of their time but did not offer you a job or recommendation. What should you do?

You follow up. Why? Because you have just created a stakeholder. A stakeholder is someone who has a stake in what you are doing. Why should someone who has offered you advice take an interest in your career? They will take interest because once they have offered you advice, their advice will contribute to your career. If you are successful, it will validate their advice.

"Hey! Thank you! Because of the advice I received from you I landed a job at...." And guess what! You have just opened the door a little wider with that person for future advice. They will undoubtedly feel that at least some of your success was due to their advice—and it probably was—so be generous with your thanks and your experience because one day you might get a similar call.

You are building your network. You will find those who are very accessible and enjoy keeping in touch and those who are not. Here lies another lesson. You are dealing with people and each is different. It is what makes life fun and interesting. If you meet someone who is helpful but seems to keep a distance, respect it, do not take it personally and thank them profusely for their help.

Develop an emotional framework that will lead to success

Are you ready for a valuable insight? Most people will fail to open this opportunity for themselves. Not because they are lazy or not interested, but simply out of fear. Fear of rejection is one of the most powerful pacifiers of all the human emotions. The best way to overcome fear is simply by picking up the telephone and calling. You'll be surprised how open and helpful most people are and how willing they are to help.

You will face rejection. There will be people who will be too busy or not interested in helping, but they will be the minority. If the first few calls do not give you the contact that you are looking for...make another telephone call. Don't take it personally. There are many reasons why someone may be unable to meet with you. Here are just a few.

1. They have a grumpy personality and even their mother would have a hard time getting them away from their office. Why would you want to meet with a person like this anyway?

2. Root canal 3 hours earlier.

3. Their spouse's divorce lawyer just called.

4. Their computer crashed, destroying the presentation they are expected to give in 15 minutes.

5. The Internal Revenue Service found a mistake and are sending a bill for $15,000.

6. His wife called and the wind ripped off their new roof, causing the rain to warp their new kitchen flooring.

7. He was just fired.

8. She really is very, very business.

9. His daughter called. She parked his car in a tow-away zone, and the car wasn't there when she returned.

10. His daughter called from Las Vegas, where she just married the surfer.

People have lives and life happens. Respect people's time as you would have them respect your time. Value their time too. When you finally get your appointment, thank the person when you meet them and send a note to them after you have left thanking them not only for their time but for their advice as well. Remember: When you get your next job or assignment be sure to call or e-mail or drop a note in the mail to thank them again for their valuable advice.

TIPS FROM THE PROS

"In my experience, the one characteristic that all excellent student portfolios share is they contain at least one truly great piece of communication. Something–that when I looked at it–I wish I had done myself. Something I wanted to take around the agency and show to people.

"Look at this."

There are other things I look for–of course. They are nothing revolutionary. I want to see strong conceptual thinking. I want to see craftsmanship–the writer kind and the art director kind. I think today's student book is better than it's ever been on the conceptual end. I also think today's student book leaves a bit to be desired on the craftsmanship end. Particularly for art directors.

Everything that's powerful about this business begins with an idea. But that said, writer's who can't write and art director's who can't art direct don't last very long. A portfolio should demonstrate an understanding of what constitutes a good idea–but also, demonstrate a respect for the craft.

If you are a writer, show me a well-constructed headline. Show me you can write body copy. Write an intelligent caption. Convince me you have a passion for the written word and that you understand the fundamentals of how the English language behaves.

If you are an art director, show me something artful. Demonstrate you have an understanding of typography. That you know how to layout and organize the printed page. That you can draw. That you have taste. Show me there is more to you than what's contained in your computer's pull-down menu.

Again, conceptual ability is the most important skill a portfolio must contain. But craftsmanship is often the difference between–at least for me–someone I'm interested in and someone I'm not.

Most good portfolios are–more than anything–the product of passion for the work. Believe it or not, you can sense that from a book. And when a creative director finds passion for the work combined with natural talent, most pick up the telephone and call the personnel department.

Trust your instincts. The best creatives in our industry are individuals who are just that–individuals. A unique voice is a good thing. Don't let art schools and award show annuals pound that out of you. Put work in your book you're proud of.

In developing your portfolio, draw inspiration from culture, not other advertising.

(continued)

> **Avoid easy subjects to create ads about. Instead, do ads for soap, cars, fast food, real things. It's more difficult. But better.**
>
> **Be honest with yourself. If you don't love doing the work–keep looking.**
>
> *Hal Curtis*
> *Creative Director*
> *Weiden + Kennedy*

FIGURE 6.3

Zave Smith is one photographer who works very aggressively on his vision and how he presents it to his audience. Every decision is carefully thought out, and the outcome is always a strong presentation. He develops his portfolio into a compelling visual narrative which is very consistent through all the media he uses.

When Bad things happen to good people

Everyone will now and then make a misstep, that's just how it is. The way to a successful career is to make as few as possible and to learn from them so you never have to make them again. If you can learn from someone else's mistake, even better. One of the signs of a great manager is to anticipate the problems his or her staff might encounter and provide them with the knowledge beforehand so they won't make any mistakes.

There are many reasons that things don't work out as you have planned. When that happens, it can be a very lonely time. It can come from a merger and reorganization, a downsizing due to a lost account, or a serious mistake that you made or one that someone else made. Whatever the reason, just when you have all of your plans in place and you think you know what is going to happen, life happens.

This is the time that the network that you built can be invaluable. They can help you focus and define the problem and hopefully help you to get back on track.

An illustrator was finishing one of the biggest assignments of his career with one of the biggest agencies in town. He returned to the agency and was surprised to find another art director on the project. The new art director saw the completed work and refused it saying simply that he hated it and would not pay for it.

The illustrator was crushed but called an associate and relayed the story. The associate referred him to a seasoned illustrator who had been in the business for many more years than the illustrator and who had also worked with the agency many times. Upon asking the senior illustrator if he would look at the work, he responded by asking to see the contract and any other papers from the agency that outlined the work, including any correspondence about the work. The illustrator luckily was one of those types who was very careful about contracts and paperwork and produced a detailed paper trail.

As they went through the paperwork, the senior member understood the assignment and only then did he ask to see the finished illustrations. After reviewing the work, he determined that the young illustrator had in fact met the objectives of the assignment and suggested that he return to the agency and meet with the art buyer and the art director to review the project. The young illustrator did and during the meeting the art director acknowledged that the illustrator had in fact met the objectives of the project and although he would have not chosen his particular style for the assignment, the illustrator's work did in fact accomplish what it was supposed to do.

There are many times in your career that you will run into a wall. The larger your network, the better chance you will have to get help getting over that wall.

You're fired

Ouch!

Even if it doesn't come from Donald Trump, those two words more than any others can be earth shattering. If you are fired from a job or off of a job, there is not a whole lot anyone can say to turn your spirits around. Sure you can lay the blame on the person who delivered the message, but it doesn't bring a lot of satisfaction no matter who you feel was responsible it is still you who is out in the street.

Manage crisis

If you are asked off a job, find out why. It may have been due to circumstances that were beyond anyone's control. The company may simply need to reduce the number of people who are working on the project. It probably won't be the best day of your life, but it doesn't have to be the worst. If you listen closely enough, it might also be a learning experience. What is it that they needed that you weren't providing?

Sometimes it can be a problem between personalities, a work deficiency, or a communications problem. It is always worthwhile to understand the real reason. It could be that the boss's wife doesn't like someone who wears black all the time. Most important, it doesn't mean that you won't be a star on your next job.

A photographer after 2 days of shooting a 5-day shoot was told that the shoot had been cancelled because the legislation that was expected to pass and was necessary for the introduction of the product did not pass and the project was shelved. The photographer had a contract with a cancellation cause and he and his crew were paid for the days he did not shoot. There were no hard feelings and he eventually worked with the client again.

An agency art director was fired because the creative director didn't feel that he was producing the type of work that the agency's clients needed. The art director who had been at the agency for about 18 months did not see this coming and was surprised by it. He felt that he was struggling with some of the accounts but felt that he was still able to sell work to his clients.

He asked for a meeting with the creative director and the human resources person in the agency. He expressed his thoughts and felt it was only a matter of time before he would have been on top of it. The creative director went through a list of examples to show the art director how his actions were seen from the other people managing the account. He listened, but more than that he asked questions that would help him better understand how he might have handled some of these situations in a better way.

The meeting lasted for about an hour and a half, at the end of which he asked for a letter of acknowledgement for future employers. The letter would say that he had worked at the agency for a certain time as an art director. He was pleasantly surprised that when he received the letter from human resources (HR), it had a positive tone never mentioning that he had been fired but stating that he was a conscience employee. He sent off a note thanking the HR manager.

A few months latter he received a call from the same HR manager. She had an opening with another creative director in the agency and was wondering if he would be interested. She said that this creative director worked more closely with his staff and she felt that he would benefit from his mentorship.

He had already taken a position at a smaller agency where he felt comfortable. They were happy with his work and he had learned a lesson from his previous position to check in regularly with his creative director. He understood how important it was to stay in touch. Six years later he was back at the previous agency as an associate creative director.

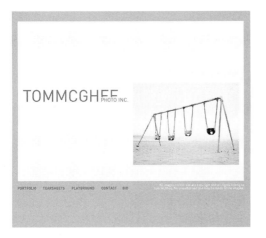

FIGURE 6.4

He is an example of two pages from photographer Tom McGhee's Web site along with one of his photographs. What is striking about his presentation is the way in which he makes the makes his work stand out. The site has limited navigation because it focuses on the clearest and fastest way to present his photographs. He also includes a section called, "Playground," which traditionally is titled personal work but Tom's description is playful and gives the viewer a better insight into his vision as an artist.

Don't burn bridges

There are only five people working in your business. Well, maybe a few more but burn a few bridges and you will very quickly how small business can be, "Oh didn't you just work with Tom? Mind if I give him a call?"

On the other hand, as part of your strategy make it a point to keep every door open. A job goes bad—ask to go out to lunch to discuss it. Tell the person you'll take them to the restaurant of their choice. Show them that you really care about resolving the problem. Maybe you won't ever work with them again but if someone happens to call them at least you have a fighting chance.

Cultivating a successful attitude means being responsive

As I was compiling this book I contacted a wide selection of professionals. I looked for people who had a definite vision, who had something to say, and whose work could inspire others. I choose people who had made their mark and people who were just starting out and had still to make their mark. Some of the latter, even though they were only beginning their career, were already starting to gain recognition. What I found was interesting and worth passing along.

On every level—from the seasoned to ones in their early careers—the people who had separated themselves from the pack when contacted responded immediately. They provided their material when they said they would and followed up to ensure it had got to me and was in a form that I needed.

There was another group that although their work was at the same level, hadn't reached the level of recognition of the first group. I found that I had to follow up with them, some several times, to remind them to forward their work.

What is the lesson here?

It's simple: Great work isn't enough. The people who distinguish themselves do so because they look for opportunities and embrace them when they find them. They are fully committed to their careers and when they make a commitment they feel a responsibility to honor it.

Those people who separate themselves may find themselves distanced from their career goal and from the people who can help them get where they want to be.

Your career is in your hands. You make the choices and your choices will determine your success.

Good luck.

YOUR ASSIGNMENT

Building your network

It is never too early or too late to compile your dream list of people who you want to meet and connect with. Your goal is to develop a contact list of around 200 names. These are people who one way or another can help you with your career.

This is a list that you will maintain throughout your entire career.

The point of this exercise is that you want to build a network of people who recognize your name and are familiar with your work. This doesn't mean that you have to call them once a day but it does mean that they should be familiar with your goals.

Now, 200 contacts might seem a daunting task, so begin with a list of 20 and add five new names each month or in a time period that you feel comfortable.

How do you find people to add to your list?

There are dozen of sources where you will be able to find people to ad to you list. Some of these are trade magazines, associations like art director's clubs, photography associations, award annuals, and community groups, but don't forget friends and family. When you do make your connection, you can also ask that person to refer another and make sure you give every person you meet your business card.

You can approach these people directly, in person, or by phone or by letter. You can begin an introduction by mentioning that you admire their work and would like to ask them some advice. Before you finish the conversation, ask them if they would mind if you contact them in the future if you have another question.

Before you know it, you will have built a list of people who you will find invaluable and over time, some of these might become good friends, have a job that is right for you, or refer you to the right job. Make sure you keep in touch with everyone on your list at least once every 90 days. It can be as simple as informing them that you just won an award or got a project or job and wanted to let them know.

It's time to begin compiling your first 20 contacts:

1. _____

Name   Title   Telephone

Address

_____

Last topic of conversation

2. _____

Name   Title   Telephone

Address

_____

Last topic of conversation

3. _____

Name   Title   Telephone

Address

_____

Last topic of conversation

4. _____

Name   Title   Telephone

Address

_____

Last topic of conversation

5. _____

Name   Title   Telephone

Address

_____

Last topic of conversation

6. _____

Name   Title   Telephone

Address

_____

Last topic of conversation

7. _____

Name   Title   Telephone

Address

_____

Last topic of conversation

8. _____

Name   Title   Telephone

Address

_____

Last topic of conversation

9. _____

Name   Title   Telephone

Address

_____

Last topic of conversation

10. _____

Name   Title   Telephone

Address

_____

Last topic of conversation

11. _____

Name   Title   Telephone

Address

_____

Last topic of conversation

12. _____

Name   Title   Telephone

Address

_____

Last topic of conversation

13. _____

Name   Title   Telephone

Address

_____

Last topic of conversation

14. _____

    Name   Title   Telephone

    Address

    _____

    Last topic of conversation

15. _____

    Name   Title   Telephone

    Address

    _____

    Last topic of conversation

16. _____

    Name   Title   Telephone

    Address

    _____

    Last topic of conversation

17. _____

    Name   Title   Telephone

    Address

    _____

    Last topic of conversation

18. _____

    Name   Title   Telephone

    Address

    _____

    Last topic of conversation

19. _____

    Name   Title   Telephone

    Address

    _____

    Last topic of conversation

20. _____

    Name   Title   Telephone

    Address

    _____

    Last topic of conversation

CHAPTER 7

The Digital Portfolio

The online portfolio **and** other digital **portfolios**

There are numerous how-to books that explain the tools you need to build a Web site; this chapter is not about how to use these tools. This chapter will examine what people are looking for in a Web site and discuss how to translate your brand or vision into a compelling Web site and other digital media.

A Web site is a great way to expose someone to your work, but it should be considered as only a part of your overall marketing strategy. If a person wants to get an idea of the type of work that you do and will not meet with you in person having them visit your URL is a quick and easy way to make an introduction. However, if someone wants to meet with you, always come prepared with a portfolio presentation—whether it is on the computer or in a book. Do not expect when you arrive at someone's office that you can go online to review your work. Why? Every company in the world has computer crashes. They don't want it, and they do everything they can to avoid it, but it happens. If you arrive at a potential client expecting to review your work with them online and their Internet connection is down you have lost an opportunity. They may also have expected that you were to bring a presentation and have arranged your meeting in a conference room without a computer. It happens all the time.

In addition if you are there, the interviewer has probably seen your work online anyway. Bringing a portfolio gives you another opportunity to show them your work in another form and delve deeper into the details of how you solve problems. You also get to show your work the way you want it viewed. This can be a powerful advantage for you. A user controls the way he/she wants to see your work on your Web site. He/she may wish to skip ahead or ignore work altogether. When you are sitting with him/her you can arrange your work to tell your complete story and fully reveal your vision.

Few people receive an assignment or get hired simply because someone visited their site. It does happen, but in most cases it is still a business where a personal connection is needed to land a job.

I made my first online portfolio in 1994. The great part of building them back then was that building and launching them became a community event.

At launch, a crowd of us would gather and patiently wait for the site to appear. The moment it launched, we would celebrate. We were doing things that not many had done before so there was great excitement when any site that you were involved with went live. The other reason was that when it finally did go live it did not always go live or at least not all of it. Many nights we huddled over each other's computers pouring over code and pulling it apart and putting it back together again, finally seeing the site launch and the sun come up.

In the end, it was a great learning experience to do this with a group who wanted to be on the edge sharing their learning and experiences. Everyone involved always gained a little more knowledge or discovered a line of code that they didn't know before.

The exhilaration of guiding someone to your URL to visit your portfolio was sometimes followed by deflation. More often than not, you would get a phone call that it crashed their computer or did not download properly. This would always be followed by, "Uh. Why don't you just send over your portfolio for us to look at?" That was the price of living on the edge.

Fast forward to today. The call you will get, will probably come because someone has looked at your Web site first.

Online portfolios are great for certain things like animation and not so great for fine detail like very fine script typography. Think carefully about which work of yours is best presented over the Web. If it is a beautiful piece of work but it doesn't represent well online, rather than compromise the portfolio you should think about showing another piece instead.

The tools available in the market for building a Web site along with the adoption rate of broadband have made it easier to build a great site and have it seen. But there are a few things to consider when developing a portfolio using digital media and we are going to look at these in this chapter.

FIGURE 7.1

Here is a beautiful site—from the illustrator Alison Stephen—that works very hard but looks effortless. When you go to her site, you are struck by the simplicity and strength of design. It feels like you are opening a page of her sketchbook. She has a wonderful loose style that she translated into the site. The navigation is her work. She know how to focus her clients on what is important to her and to them, The site was so simple and so beautifully done that I spent more time getting involved with her work. Of course, that's exactly what she wanted me to do.

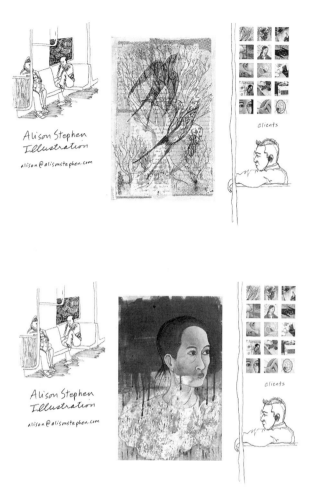

What makes a great site

A Web site is one part of your total presentation. The framework for a site starts back in Chapter 2 where we discussed creating your vision. The site should emerge from the attributes and promise that you developed.

One of the wonderful attributes that the Web has over other media is that is a terrific media for storytelling. You are a storyteller of your own story. When you are building your site, consider how you want your story to unfold.

When thinking about an online portfolio one of the first solutions that designers usually consider is building the site in flash. While flash is a great program and is evolving into an even better program every year, there are some things to think about. Flash is not searchable, so if it is important for the search engines to find your site, you may want to find another solution. For example, if you build in Flash you might want to include a footer outside Flash that can be recognized by search engines. (As the Flash program is further developed it will no doubt introduce properties that will allow anything developed in the program to be searchable.)

Flash is good if you have images on your site that you want to protect. It is difficult for someone to copy your image when it is embedded in flash. This is something that might be of interest to illustrators and photographers to protect their copyrighted images.

Splash pages are great fun to build and share with friends. However, think carefully about your end user—will they be amused if the have to sit through 45 seconds of animation to get into your site.

If you built it on a MAC, did you look at your site on a PC? Don't assume that everyone looking at your site is MAC based. How does your site look on different browser settings? Does it work on all of them? Does it need to work on all of them?

Most people find the building of a Web site a daunting task. They liken it to rolling a large heavy ball up the side of a mountain. What we want to do is take the mountain out of the way. There is still a lot of work that has to be accomplished but it doesn't have to be an uphill struggle. This book has been set up to help you develop a system that will help lead you step by step. There may be choices to consider but there are always clear steps to support your forward progress.

One of the biggest challenges people seem to face is knowing when their Web site is finished. Unfortunately, a good site is never finished—it is continually in the process of evolution. For example, if you are a designer and want to convince your audience that you are on the leading edge of technology there are great tools out there to create an awe inspiring Web site. However 6 months from now if your potential clients are returning to your site and it isn't reflecting the latest advancements they will look elsewhere for a designer that has used them.

A photographer wants to update his or her images to keep the site fresh and encourage art buyers to return to view the latest work.

One solution that a number of people are using is the, "new work," button in the navigation. This immediately guides your clients to your latest and greatest and because it is limited to one portion of your site, it is easily updated.

TIPS FROM THE PROS

"My job is to actualize an art director's vision. When I look for a photographer, I look for someone who understands where the cutting edge is and is able to bring their work there without compromising their vision.

I often refer to Web sites, but if I like the work I will always call in the portfolio. There is a big difference when looking at work at 72 dpi and then seeing it printed in a portfolio. I also enjoy seeing how the artist handles the work on the page as well as their selection of paper that they chose for their work."

Diane Kirkwood
Art Buyer
Grey Advertising
New York

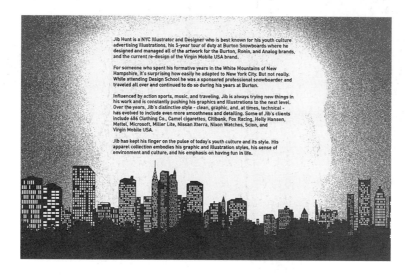

FIGURE 7.2

Jib Hunt is an illustrator, and designer. He also
has developed a market for himself designing
and selling t-shirts. The t-shirts can be found on
his Web site and promote his work while
producing revenue.

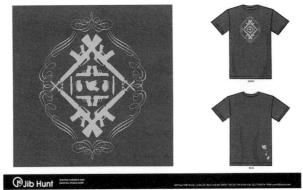

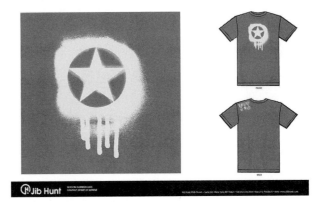

15 X 21 POSTER

GIFT OF PURCHASE: CUSTOM JIB HUNT DOG TAG WITH 30" CHAIN COMES WITH EVERY T-SHIRT

To Splash or not to splash

The Web is about turning choices over to the user. They decide what they want to see and when they want to see it. They are the navigators of your site, not you. The days of forcing someone to sit through some animation before they enter your site are over. No one wants to waste their time looking at something they don't want to see. If animation is an important part of your offering a better solution is to dedicate a section of your home page to preview animation clips so your viewer can decide what is important to him/her. Maybe the viewer just wants to get your telephone number and may not wait through 45 seconds of animation to get it. One solution around this it is to use a "skip intro" command or find another way to show the animation.

There are sites having a fabulous piece of animation to introduce them that are stronger than any of the work shown. It gives the impression that someone else did the animation and this may not leave the best impression for the viewer about you or your work. Any animation should support your vision and brand and not overpower it.

FIGURE 7.3

Here is the home page for Patrick Dorian's Web site along with some samples of his work. This is an effective home page. The navigation is easy to follow and his product, his illustrations, are the highlight of the site. He has localized his animation so the site is able to load quickly. The animation that he does have on his site supports his vision while being playful and quite engaging.

Landing pages and why they should be avoided

Another annoyance is "the click here to enter the site" direction. If the viewer has already typed in the URL to be directed to the site, why should he or she be taken to a landing page that requests another action to gain access to the site? Make it simple, make it easy, and make it fast for the user. They want to get the information they want without going places that don't get them to it.

The "I don't trust you, so agree to this before you can come in" link

Please agree to my terms before I will let you enter my site. Some photographers and image creators believe that it adds a level of protection for them if they have visitors agree to their terms before they let them onto the site. An example is "the images on this site are copyrighted and any infringement will ...." First, this is not a user-friendly act and second a professional image maker should have copyrighted all the images on the site before launching it. The copyright would afford the creator of the images complete protection with the weight of copyright infringement laws behind him or her. If you feel it is important to draw their attention to the copyright simply place a copyright symbol on the work or the page or a line on the site stating that everything is copyrighted.

You want to make your information accessible and easy to find while giving the visitor an enjoyable experience.

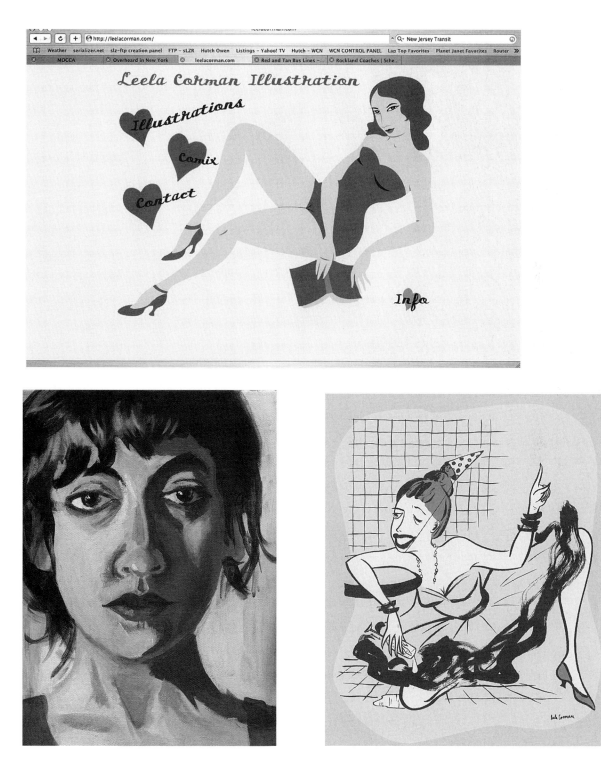

FIGURE 7.4

Leela Corman's home page to her Web site is deceptively simple. It contains an illustration, her name, and four navigation buttons. Although her illustrations appear very playful, it is not until further investigation that what is revealed is her mature handling of the subject matter. Upon visiting her work, the illustration on the home page begins to reveal more secrets.

FIGURE 7.5

"Stinky Pickles" is one of Leela Corman's graphic stories. Like all her work it is not what it first appears to be but clearly reflects her vision.

Does your Web site need to be found by the search engines?

There are two questions to examine. First, does your Web site need to be found by the search engines? Second, does the product that you are producing need to be found by the search engines?

While the Flash program offers some challenges for the search engines they are becoming more clever in their way to "read" Flash. There are several ways to get the most from the search engines. The first, of course, is to register your site with them providing a list of services as keywords, An html header or footer is a good way to help your sites be recognized by the search engines. Another important technique is to tag all of your imagery with keywords. For example if I am preparing a jpeg image for my site I would name it Thurlbeck_Ken_Portrait_6.jpg. When a search engine is trolling you have 2 chances to be seen, once by your name and again by what you do.

Some domain registries and domain hosts will automatically register you when you sign with them. Ask about their policy beforehand and be prepared to follow up yourself with the search engines. Google and their competitors are aggressively changing the search landscape almost daily. Once still images and video were not searchable but today they are so it is important when naming your images to embed keywords that will give you the response you desire.

Decide what is important to you when you are building a site. Make a list before you choose the tools and programs you will use. Look carefully at each of them and what they will do for you and what they won't. It is better to understand this before you begin building your site. If you are using a designer do the same with him or her. Make a list of what you need from your site then figure out what and how you need to build it.

A few more simple guidelines

blueelephantswimingiinthenile.com may be an interesting and creative URL but will it be memorable? The industry standard is 8/3, which means an eight-or-less–letter name followed by .com. If it is possible to keep your URL shorter, it helps the viewer to remember it. If you are your brand you might want to use your own name or part of it. This way if someone is looking for you, they can try your name in the URL or use your name to find you with a search engine.

The most prized spot for the highest recall on a Web page is the upper left-hand corner. It also is one of the few places on a page that is always visible when a page loads. Designs that place the name of the site and navigation at the bottom of a page create a design that might hide those elements, depending the user's browser's settings. It is the same as navigation on the right side of the page. Depending upon how the page is built, the navigation might fall off of the page.

Whenever possible you want to keep information above the fold. What that means is that if you have a lot of information on a page and the page runs off the bottom of the browser window, the users will have to scroll down the page to retrieve the information. If it is necessary to run a longer page, make sure that the scroll bar is easy to find. It is also helpful in these cases to keep the important information above the fold or near the top of the page. This will ensure that if the visitor doesn't have the time or desire to scroll through your all of your information, he or she will at least see what is important.

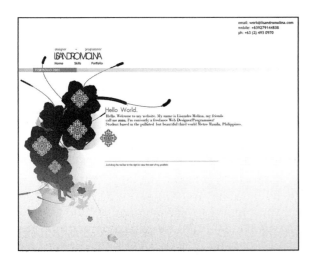

FIGURE 7.6

Designer Lisandro Molina has a site that is very engaging. The navigation is a red bar that, when pulled across the site, reveals the portfolio section. The design of the site captures the designer's sensibilities and communicates it clearly to the viewer.

If you want a visitor to return to your home page, make certain that you provide a link to get them there, but don't put a home page link on your home page. Your visitor is already there.

Everything you can possibly think of sometimes should *not* be in your site

Some sites may have seemed like good ideas at the time they were developed but when launched didn't get the desired response. For example, if you have an interesting design that buries the navigation and the visitor has to spend more than 15 seconds to find it, you may lose him or her. This doesn't mean that you have to lose a great idea, but it does mean you need to discover a system that will incorporate your ideas and load fast. It means a clear and easy-to-use navigation system that gets the user to where they want to go quickly. It should be fun because the more you can engage your user, the *stickier* your site will be. A sticky site is a site that engages the user longer.

Preloading versus streaming

If you have a site that is heavy with design or image elements, you can have a preloader on your site. The preload will load all the images so that once a viewer is into the site he or she will not have to wait to review the work. The other choice to consider is to stream the images so that they will load when the person views them. Some believe that preloading a site will cause the viewer to leave if it takes too long, whereas others believe that once a user is into the site, he or she will not mind waiting for a streaming image.

There is no rule of thumb and because broadband is reaching more customers, downloading is becoming less of an issue. You can be fairly certain that all the businesses you are contacting are working with systems that offer fast downloads. The main consideration is to keep your images as light as possible by optimizing them so the file sizes will be as small as possible.

How to generate hits

There is a misconception that the more hits your site gets, the better it is. It isn't hits you want but qualified hits. This is a principle that people are now just beginning to really understand. A *qualified hit* is a hit that leads you to a job, an assignment, or a business transaction.

You can set up a links page on your site and develop relationships with other sites to list your links. There are many sites looking for this type of relationship. Listing on numerous sites will no doubt increase the number of hits your site gets, but will the people who hit your site be the type of people that will buy your service? Choose wisely. It is better to be very selective and direct the traffic that can benefit you than to cast a wide net that will offer no value to you.

FIGURE 7.7

Frank Veronsky has made a reputation for himself by making unconventional and compelling photographs for the past 16 years. His site supports this vision with an unconventional but engaging presentation. It not only shows his work and his thinking but demonstrates that he applies his unique vision to everything he gets involved with.

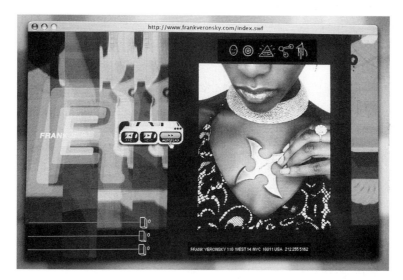

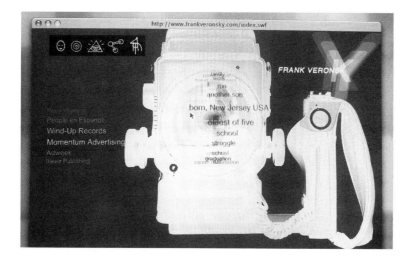

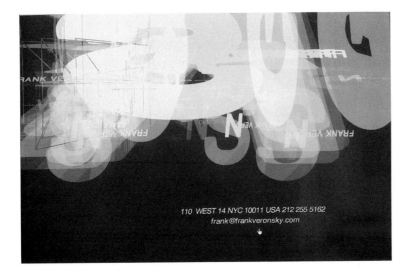

110 WEST 14 NYC 10011 USA 212 255 5162
frank@frankveronsky.com

CDs/DVDs

Any presentation or presentation format should be user friendly. Writing a CD or DVD that has an elaborate or unclear navigational system or requires the user to dig through folders should be avoided. A clear plug and play is desirable.

DVDs have been more successful than CDs at achieving better performance, but the two still can present problems. In most companies, the administration side of the company is PC-based whereas the creative side uses MACs. It is necessary to test your finished presentation on both formats before assuming it will work on both. One problem remains and that is the "cranky" nature of people's systems. More times than not, I have seen someone arrive to show their work bringing only a CD and have the CD crash the system or simply not open. DVDs work a little better in that regard but it depends on the programs that were used to construct the presentations.

Unless there is a very good reason to develop your presentation on these formats, I would recommend that you understand how you want to use these and work with the tools that will make them acceptable to the end user. Animation or motion is a reason to use a DVD format, but only if you have the ability to make it trouble-free. I use a DVD to showcase my television commercial work and most of the industry now uses this standard but it is plug and play. My Web work also uses a DVD format, but I remember crashing client's systems with CD-ROMs.

What ever you decide, test it, test it, and test it before using it in a presentation.

Shaped CDs and DVDs should be avoided. They are an interesting conversation piece but do not hold a lot of information and can get stuck in someone's computer, especially MACs. The business card CD that looks like a business card with slightly rounded corners can be printed as a business card on one side and burned as a CD on the other. I have seen this derail presentations and leave a room full of people looking at a frozen screen.

Thumb Drives, iPods, and ...

I like to be prepared. Whenever I am presenting work I like to have a backup. A thumb drive is a great way to carry information. I find it helpful as well to carry a listing of the most current URLs that I am working on. This way I can show someone the latest work even before I have posted it onto my site. My television commercial director's reel is copied on to my iPod, which I take everywhere. It has proven invaluable many times when I have had impromptu meeting with prospective clients and friends.

Many formats are available to present your work. Use them creatively and keep watching for the next format that will catch someone's attention. At the moment, I am wondering how I can use a cell phone to present a portfolio. Maybe you'll show me.

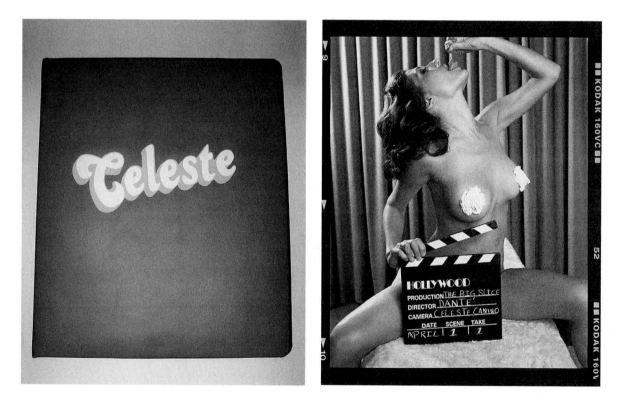

FIGURE 7.8

I was reunited with Celeste at a photographer's portfolio review at the art director's club in New York. Several years earlier, she was my West Coast representative and when I returned to the East Coast, I had lost touch with her. Four years ago, Celeste realized that she belonged behind the camera and from that moment on she has focused on a career as a photographer. When I saw her portfolio and her Web site, I was excited to see that she had done it right. Her work and its presentation are consistent, delightful, and totally focused. Everything about her work pushes the edge with a wonderful sense of humor. Here is the cover to her book with some of her images.

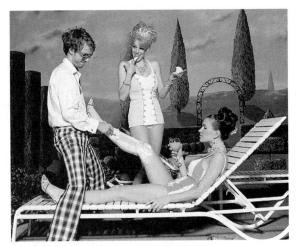

FIGURE 7.9

Whether you look at her portfolio, her Web site, or her promotional material, there is a single and strong visual narrative. Her Web site is tightly edited to keep the viewer engaged and amused.

The site map

The better your site is organized, the more successful it will be. So before you even begin thinking about the design you should develop a site map. The site map is a schematic organizational chart that helps you decide where everything goes on your site and how the user will navigate through the site to get there. Is there a need for subnavigation? If you are a photographer, you may want to direct your visitors to your photographs of people. Your navigation might begin with a portfolio button, which might lead the user to choose from landscapes, still life, and people. The people tab when clicked may offer the user three additional choices for example men, women, and children. Your main navigation should be limited to no more than eight buttons. All of these choices should be defined in your site map. The site map is the skeleton from which your site will emerge.

Once you have a workable site map, you are well on your way to a finished site. The site map is also a great starting point for a CD-ROM or DVD.

Now let's look at applying some of the ideas from this chapter.

YOUR ASSIGNMENT

Your Web site

There are many tools to use and ways to build your Web site but what every way you decide to go there are a few basic steps that you will have to consider.

The assignment here is to organize the information you will use to bring your brand and vision to life on your Web site.

Site map and site organization

This is where you start to organize and lay out your site. Is the navigation clear and is there a systematic order to the way the pages work with your navigation.

Design a site map. Does the navigation follow an intuitive logic? How many pages are necessary to present your information and is it possible to combine pages? Does adding additional levels of navigation help the organization of the site?

The color palette

You have developed a color palette in chapter 2 now you want to develop a color palette for your Web site and develop a system to use it.

Primary color and secondary and tertiary colors should be considered into a system that will help lead the user through your site. For example how the color works with your navigation and roll-overs. Do you change the color for each level of navigation? Do you use color to identify the different levels or pages in the site.

I love peanut butter but have a hard time finding the right mixture between crunchy and smooth so I buy both and mix them to my desired consistency when I spread them onto bread. I mentioned this because of the color system used by the peanut butter manufacturer. The lid of the smooth peanut butter jar is a lighter blue while the lid of the chunky is a darker blue. The lid of the super chunky is a deep dark blue. This is a system that makes logical sense. The lighter the color of the lid, the lighter and smoother the peanut butter. The chunkier the peanut butter the heavier and richer the color of the lid. It is very intuitive and so should your use of color.

Develop a color palette beginning with your basic brand colors. Consider how you will use the colors for navigation, identification of pages, roll-overs etc.

Apply these colors to your site map. Are the colors used consistently throughout the site?

Typography

Your typography should now be determined from the work that you did earlier but does it work on your Web site? If you are hard coding the site and you used a serif type, can you use a similar typeface that is more universally recognized by the Web? If you have used a fine serif or script how does it translate? You may want to make a JPEG of a finely detailed logo or signature.

You will have navigation, body copy, headlines on your site. Look at all the copy on your site and assign type styles to each. Take this information and place it on to a typography standards sheet. This will be your style guide for your site.

Wire frames and real estate

Wire frames are a good way to start looking at the layout for each page or combination of pages. It will help you organize your information and decide what is important. One way to begin this is to list all the items on a page and numerically categorize which is the most important to which is least important. At that point you can, much like dividing up a parcel of land, designate which item you want to give more space to and which you want to give less to.

What is the most important thing that you want to communicate on a page. This piece of information should get the most attention, best position or biggest space.

This is where you want to organize your pages. Which pages are similar in layout and which require different layouts. The more pages that share the same layout the easier it will be to build the site.

Design and layout a wire frame for each different page type.

Navigation

Navigation should be simple and straight forward. It does not have to be the standard, "portfolio about me." It can be fun, engaging, and personalized but it needs to be clear enough to move your viewer to where they want to go.

So have some fun with it.

Name your navigation buttons and design a rollover state for them. Do this for all navigation layers.

Now you are ready to design your site. Send me your URL, I can't wait to see it.

Resources

Off-the-Shelf Premade Portfolios

Pearl Paint: www.pearlpaint.com
Print File: 1 800 508-8539; www.printfilw.com
Nicole Anderson Book Arts: www.nabookarts.com
House of Portfolios: 52 West 21st St. NYC NY 10010; (t) 212 206-7323;
www.houseofportfolios.com
Lost Luggage: (t) 888-lost456; www.lost-luggage.com
Kolo Books: available at Barnes & Noble, Borders, Plaza Art and
www.artsuppliesonline.com
Light Impressions: 439 Monroe Avenue Rochester, NY 14603; (t) 800 828-6216
Brewer-Cantelmo: 350 Seventh Ave. NY, NY 10001 (t) 212 244-4600;
www.brewer-cantelmo.com
Kate's Paperie: 561 Broadway, NYC, NY 10012 (t) 212 941-9816;
www.katespaperie.com
Molly West Handbound Books: 1255 A Park Avenue, Emeryyville, CA 94608;
(t) 510 653-2830; www.mollywest.com

Custom Portfolios

Mario Acerboni: Via Mattei, 14(Zona Ind.) 25060 Collebeato Brescia, Italy;
(t) (39) 030 2511345, (f) (39) 030 2510101; www.marioacerbonialbum.it
Brewer-Cantelmo: 350 Seventh Ave. NYC, NY 10001; (t) 212 244-4600;
www.brewer-cantelmo.com
House of Portfolios: 52 West 21st St. NYC NY 100010; (t) 212 206-7323;
www.houseofportfolios.com
Lost Luggage: (t) 888-lost456; www.lost-luggage.com
Advertisers Display Binder: 195 New York Avenue, Jersey City, NJ 07307;
(t) 201 795 3515; www.adbportfolio.com; Canada (t) 1800 661 6849
Roswell Bookbinding: 2614 North 29th Ave., Phoenix, AZ. 85009; (t) 602 272-
9338
Custom Presentations: 214 939-2300
Minnesota Center for Book Arts: 1011 Washington Avenue, Suite 100,
Minneapolis, MN 55415; (t) 612 215-2520

Custom Bindery & Specialties: 1316 S. Tyron St., Charlotte, NC 28237-7308;
(t) 704 322-2195
Talas: 568 Broadway NYC 10012, 212 219 0770; www.talasonline.com
Free Guerrilla Marketing Ideas: This is a site that offers crisply written marketing ideas from the authors of a book called Guerrilla Marketing. Lots of insights
and tough talk. See for yourself at www.gmarketing.com
Free fax to your E-Mail: Always a handy device. www.efax.com. You download
software to convert faxes directly into email messages. It's magic and you are
guaranteed to get a personal fax number with a weird area code. Nonetheless it
will let you receive faxes remotely and with high resolution.

Connect to your community

www.adweek.com

wwww.adage.com

www.marketingclick.com

www.brandera.com

www.clickz.com

www.commarts.con

www.pdnonline.com

www.printmag.com

www.hintmag.com

www.craigslist.org

Gossip and information on media companies

www.vault.com

www.firmlist.com

Gossip

www.drudgereport

Help setting up a business

www.v2score.org

www.sba.gov/starting

Free Images

www.istockphoto.com

www.freeimages.co.uk

www.photodisc.com

Organizations

Art Director's Club of New York: www.adcny.org

Advertising Photographers of America: www.apa.org

Editorial Photographers: www.editorialphoto.com

Association of Media Photographers: www.asmp.org

Association of Graphic Designers

Director's Guild of America: www.dga.org

Society of Illustrators: www.societyillustrators.org

Images

www.corbis.com

www.gettyimages.com

www.photos.com

www.theispot.com/stock

www.visualsymbols.com

www.wonderfile.com

www.istockphoto.com

www.masterfile.com

www.comstock1700k.com

www.uppercutimages.com

E-zines and e-resources

Art in context: www.artincontext.org

Art support: www.art-support.com

Artist Register: www.artistregister.com

The Digital Journalist: www.digitaljournalist.com

Digital Photographer: www.digitalphotographer.net

En Foco: www.enfoco.com

Fotophile: www.fotophile.com

Journal E: www.journale.com

Fire Storm: www.firestorm.com

Photo Box: www.photobox.sk

PhotoBetty: www.photobetty.com

Santa Fe Center for Visual Arts: www.photoprojects.com

Visual Trends: www.visualtrends.com

Zone Zero: www.zonezero.com

Online Portfolios

Altpicks.com

Apanational.org (click on the portfolio search)

Commarts.com

Photoserve.com

Wookbook.com

Digital Portfolios

www.livebooks.com

www.bludomain.com

Papers for printing

Inkjet

www.hahnemuhle.com

www.epson.com

www.lumijet.com

Specialty papers

www.artsuppliesoonline.com

www.pearlpaint.com

www.handmadepapers.biz

www.custompaper.com

www.thepapercatalog.com

www.ztapdesigns.com

www.hollanders.com

www.paperhead.com

www.handmadepapers.emerchantpro.com

www.wolf-gordon.com (vinyl-backed wallpaper)

Magazines (here are some; there are a lot more)

American Photo

Art in America

BIG

Black and White

Communication Arts

Create

Flash

Graphics

Graphis

How

Photo District News

Print

The Gallery Guide

Zoom

Some fun

www.ea.com

www.spikything.com

Your Resources

Here is a good place to begin your very own resource center.

_____

_____

_____

Index